Turn Up the Lamp

First published in 1980 by

Appletree Press Ltd
The Old Potato Station
14 Howard Street South
Belfast BT7 1AP
Tel: +44 (0) 28 9024 3074
Fax: +44 (0) 28 9024 6756
E-mail: reception@appletree.ie
Web Site: www.irelandseye.com

Editor: Jean Brown
Designer: Stuart Wilkinson
Production Manager: Paul McAvoy

A catalogue record for this book is available from the British Library.

Turn Up the Lamp

ISBN: 0 86281 926 1

9 8 7 6 5 4 3 2 1

AP3202

Turn Up the Lamp

J.S. Doran

Appletree Press

Contents

Foreword

Master Joe Doran, a Mourne man born and bred, taught for many years in a country school under Slieve Binnian and knows the Kingdom of Mourne and its people well. He himself is known far outside Mourne for his poems, his stories and in particular for his books, *My Mourne* and *Hill Walks in the Mournes*. The present publication will add to his reputation and deserves to be widely read.

Turn Up the Lamp is a most refreshing account of his boyhood in Kilkeel and throws a clear light on daily life and seasonal activities in and around that market town and fishing port during and after the first World War. His home territory, as he says, measures only some six square miles – its limits determined mainly by walking distances – but it is bounded on the one side by the beckoning mountains and on the other by the sea, both providing a temptation for adventure and spur to the imagination. Incidents and accidents cutting into the routine of daily life are vividly recalled, but what gives the book its special flavour is the author's acute observation and sharp recollection of the people and places around him in his childhood, told entirely without malice and with deep affection. It makes an original and unassuming contribution to local social history as seen not from the big house or through thc ycs of the visitor but from ground level. How much richer and deeper our knowledge of the Ulster heritage would be if earlier generations had left us similar unaffected accounts of their work and play, of their physical and social environments. Mr Doran's loyalty to his home town and countryside and all their people is a shining example of good citizenship. He has unwittingly followed the advice of John Ruskin: 'Cherish above all things,' he counselled, 'local associations and hereditary skills.'

I like, for example, his description of the role played by the cobbler's shop as a quiet meeting-place for the exchange of news and general discussion. Or his account of the ecological relationships (he uses more homely terms) of the seasonal succession of youngsters' games and pastimes, and of the farmers' fairs and fishermen's fortunes. He shows that the bonds of place and community can be stronger than the sectarian ties which have so often disturbed the peace in Ulster. As a geographer, I see this as an aspect of the spirit of place, related to the circumstances of life in a well-defined geographical region – the Kingdom of Mourne – but when I wrote my *Mourne Country* I little thought that my thesis would be supported and so clearly illuminated by Joe Doran's *Turn Up the Lamp*.

E. Estyn Evans

1

The Square

With two notable exceptions each day of my life until I was fourteen was spent in and close to Kilkeel. In common with nearly all the children of the place my activities were confined to an area of little more than six square miles. Our bay bounded it a mile to the east and we seldom strayed beyond an imaginary boundary line a couple of miles to the landward side. This line was about midway between the town's little market square and the lovely arm of the mountain range. The square was the very heart of the town and the focal point for most of its youngsters.

For me it was the best place in the world to live. All streets converged there and it was seldom without traffic. That is not to say that there ever was congestion or any danger of being run down. On Fair Days, the Twelfth of July, the Fifteenth of August, St Patrick's Day or when a circus parade passed down the river brae it was, as they said, 'brave and throng', but for the rest of the year there was ample room. On monthly Fair Days (the last Wednesday of each month) or weekly flax markets (in season) the brae was seldom without a horsedrawn stiff cart. Sometimes there would be a line of five or six of them, tackling the slope at the same time, zig-zagging to make it easier as they toiled to their unharnessing placcs in the upper Courthouse square, or on the street opposite the First Presbyterian Church, or 'Big Meeting', as it was called.

The carters usually sat on cross boards when travelling light but when the vehicles were loaded with pink sucking piglets, calves or lambs, the drivers walked alongside. As they breasted the brae they appreciated a helping hand from anybody who was about. It was customary for adult pedestrians or able young grals of fellows to push from behind while the farmer trotted alongside his horse, encouraging, threatening, cajoling his straining animal to renewed efforts.

Stone carts from the granite-dressing sheds at the foothill cottages regularly hauled their loads of cribben and square sets down Mountain Road, quickening speed on the flat to provide impetus to take the sharp hill and swing left, at right angles, to the shore road. Having reached the road to the harbour the going was easier all the way to the quay where the carters tipped the loads of road-paving blocks. In time the granite was loaded on to the sailing schooners for delivery in Lancashire, South Wales and London. One side of narrow Mountain Road was, on Fair Days, always lined with carts, tipped back, their shafts pointing skywards like burp guns. Sometimes the horses were stabled in nearby yards; sometimes, when the weather was good, they were tethered to the butts of bushes that overhung one side of the little street and kept happy with nosebags of oats and windlins of straw.

Occasionally town boys who were not afraid of horses could earn a penny or two looking after the animals for farmers whose stays in the town were to be brief. Experienced lads knew that a fellow had to be choosy whom he worked for lest he finish up with a pat on the head or a couple of brandy ball sweets for his trouble instead of hard cash to buy a penn'orth of glassy marbles or a stick of liquorice from wee Mrs Mitchell.

The men who used Mountain Road while they sold their sheep or 'bastes' on the front street found it an excellent hitching place. As well as being quiet it gave access, by a common back entry and big yard, to the rear of three public houses that faced on the market square. Thus they could dovetail business with pleasure by competing their deals on the front street, entering the pubs by the front doors and, having partaken liquid refreshment, proceeding through the back doors to where their horses waited. There were fifteen public houses in the town in pre-war days and there is no record that any of them were forced to close for lack of business.

My knowledge of what went on in licensed premises was gleaned from quick glances as doors swung open. It never occurred to me that women went into the places and I was astonished the first time I saw a lady entering a public house. I stopped near the door to wait for a chance to see how she fared in this noisy man's place. The door winked open and shut a few times and then stayed open to allow me to see her sitting alone in a little glassed-in place away from the bar where men were standing two deep, glasses raised, laughing and slapping once another on the shoulders. She looked like a country woman and I supposed the man was her husband. As I looked in he came away from the bar and walked to the small room with two glasses of whiskey. He held one out to her, sat down and I heard him saying that she should drink it up for it would keep the 'hate' in her.

At the age of seven I got a chance to have a long look into a bar for the first time. I was making my usual daily call at the back door of the house where we bought our milk. Johnny, our supplier, was a farmer as well as a publican, who kept half a dozen cows in the yard at the back of his public house. It was always his wife who poured our milk from a big enamel jug into my can with its tightly fitting lid. One day I went up the back as usual but, though I knocked several times, nobody came. Consumed with curiosity I pushed the door open a foot and looked into the sparkling kitchen. There was not a sound except the tick of the big clock that stood against the wall and the singing of the iron kettle on the range. After standing for a long time I tiptoed across to the door on the other side of the kitchen and gave another knock but there was silence.

I inched open the door that led to the hall and stairs. Just at my left hand was another door, slightly open. Because of the smell that came through, I knew it was the bar. I risked pulling it a little further open. It looked as if there was nobody there. I could hear Johnny's voice from the porch at the front of the shop. Then, about half way down the long counter I saw a man on a high stool. He looked like a fisherman for he had a peaked cap, blue jersey and bell mouth trousers. His beard and moustache were very black. He did not know I was there, and I watched him looking at the huge glass of black liquid in front of him. He picked up a pepper duster that was beside him and gave it a few shakes on the creamy foam on top of the drink. He tapped the side of the glass and then lifted it to his lips. I thought he would never stop swallowing. When he put the drink down again the creamy top had lowered well down the glass. I saw clearly the lacy white frill on his moustache. Then he projected his lower lip and removed it. I heard Johnny coming into the bar from the porch and darted back to my place. I had hardly settled before his wife came down the stairs to the hall and into the kitchen. She filled my can, put the twopence in the pocket of her white apron and enquired about my mother and great-grandfather.

It took only a few minutes for me to run from Johnny's back door to our house across the brae, facing Mountain Road. Occasionally the temptation to stop for a look through the big window of the shop opposite the entry was strong enough to hold me back, especially if Stanley, the bicycle man, was at work on an upended machine. He did not mind my going in and up the long passage to his workshop, although there were hard words at home if I held back the tea. My mother, knowing my inclination to dally, usually came to the door of our two storey house, from where she could see straight up Mountain Road. If there was something on the fire that needed her attention, and there was no sign of me, my great-grandfather was sent out to see what was keeping me.

My great-grandfather had lived with us in our house on the square for as long as I could remember. Though very old (over ninety, my mother said) he was very sprightly, and I never remember him being ill. I owe my love of reading to him too, for even before I learnt to read, he allowed me to handle his books and told me about them. When not stepping about, or deep in a book, he used to snooze in his big chair at the fire with his red silk handkerchief over his head and eyes. He was well known in the town, and had regular visitors. These he always took into our front room where they talked and smoked their pipes. His favourite visitor was a big, black-dressed man who was called the curate. Any time I went into the room they were talking about horses, and the curate himself always arrived at our house on a horseback. If the doctor who lived 'over the bridge' paid a visit there was more talk of horses for, as my great-grandfather told me, the doctor was one of the leading members of the hunt that was based on Mourne Park, a few miles out of the town.

It was after the doctor's visit, when I had measles, that I heard my grandfather telling my mother that the doctor had been very upset by something that had happened at the hunt a few days before. He told her that the farmers between Mourne Park and the shore of Millbay, where the hunt finished, did not mind the horses crossing their land and jumping their ditches as long as they kept clear of cropped fields and farmyards. To make sure that this happened and that the hounds went in the right direction the men who laid the trail, pulling dead rabbits after them as they trotted across the country, stuck to the waste land and meadows. On the last hunt they had not done so but had, when approaching the yard of a well known farmer, circled the place in ever narrowing circles, finishing at the half door before lifting their rabbits and heading straight for Millbay. When the hounds arrived they too circled and closed in crashing into the door and baying with such ferocity that the farmer shot home the bolts and let the huntsmen know what he thought of them from the safety of his kitchen. My grandfather was very annoyed when telling my mother about the incident but, when he went out, I saw her smiling to herself.

On market and fair days our little streets were crowded with farm horses and carts. In the big stable yards behind the public houses the dealers from outside the district sold their animals to the country men. We were much more interested in the horse sales than in the dealing that went on in cattle, sheep and pigs on display along the sides of the streets. The hand slapping, the offers, the walking away and the arguments in the stable yards were fiercer than elsewhere. I never knew why buyers opened horses' mouths and looked in while the dealing went on. Between fairs we were always interested in the work of two clever horse trainers, or breakers, who trained young animals for saddle, cart or plough. One of the trainers, from Annalong, was a great favourite of mine. A small, tight man, just like a jockey, he was always neatly dressed in check cap and jacket, riding breeches, gleaming leggings and boots. When breaking in young animals he walked along the side of the street, the nervous animals prancing and side-stepping at the ends of long reins. He welcomed meeting groups of people, carts, bicycles and especially a chugging motor car or noisy motor cycle. It was good training for his young horse if, during his progress up the brae to the upper square, he met the big steam engine puffing and crunching into town with its load of bricks and timber.

After the fairs unsold horses were roped together and driven off on the long road journeys to other fairs or farms. Cattle that had been purchased by outside buyers were herded along the coast roads to the Greenore paddle steamer or the railway station fourteen miles away. The drovers with their strange accents were well known to all. They spent their lives walking the roads all over the counties, and were reputed to be tireless.

There was no more perfect place for watching the goings-on in the fair than the square, but nearly as important for me was the fact that, from the time I had enough teeth to deal with a caramel there was a sweet shop next door to our house. No sweet shop in my experience since has ever come up to the one in the square. It was not very big but it was packed. The mixture of smells that wafted out when you opened the door was nearly better than the treasure displayed on the shelves. There were gums, caramels in bright papers and unwrapped sugar sticks, golden sugary candy broken into lumps, paper packages with tubes of liquorice sticking out of the corners for sucking up the sharp-sweet powder, cubes of dark chocolate and chocolate bars in shiny coloured wrappers and boxes of chocolate with ribbons and pictures on the top. On the glass case on top of the counter rows of bottles of minerals were set out, some brown stoneware with spring tops, some blackish green and some clear glass with lemonade, yellow and bright, showing through.

Sunday mornings, likewise, are not a patch on those I spent just before starting school. There was hardly ever a soul to be seen on River Hill or Mountain Road half an hour before noon. When I went out on the little square of packed earth in front of our door to look around, even the street corners that usually had a few loungers were deserted. The 'Big Meeting' people would soon be walking up the hill to their place of worship; the second Mass people were well on their way on their two mile walk to Massforth, and the 'Church ones' (Church of Ireland) were being summoned from the belfry that could be seen from our door, projecting skywards above the three-pub rampart. The quick clanging bell from Christ church and the cawing of the host of rooks in the tall trees behind it are abiding memories of my summer Sunday mornings. I have to listen hard now for either bell or rooks even on the stillest day.

Bell or no bell, I always headed for Tessie's half-glassed double door. The brass latch polished by a thousand thumbs was a fitting 'open sesame'. The perfect aromatic blend of chewy things is with me still. Tessie always gave me my pick, a selection which invariably included a few butternuts, each a mouthful, thickly coated with the finest sugar and buttery enough to loosen a flood of mouth juices.

Not all my memories of the house on the square are as joyful as those in which Tessie figures. My fear of animals, for instance, I have always blamed on a terrifying experience with Johnny's goat. Johnny was the publican-farmer who lived across the brae from us. Each morning he headed his milk cows down the back entry on to Mountain Road, round the corner and up the street to the head of the town where his fields were. There was no danger to life or limb for the cows because there were no cars, and if a bicycle or a cart happened along, the cattle had right of way.

Johnny must have believed, along with everybody else in town, that goat's milk had special nutritive qualities, for he always kept a fine long-horned nanny who led the way each morning as the stock went to pasture.

One day he had stopped to talk to a neighbour. I advanced to the edge of the hill as the goat drifted over to my side of the street, and had no fear of her for I had seen her often and she had ignored me. I was not to know that this morning something had upset her. Perhaps the colour of my jersey and pants aggravated her annoyance. Anyway she closed the gap and, though I put out my hand in friendship, she would have none of it. Purposefully she lowered her huge horns and hooked me so accurately between jersey and shirt that later examination revealed that I was neither scratched nor punctured. That did not quell my terror as she reared and lifted me from the ground. The game was to her fancy and she did it again before Tessie, Johnny, my great-grandfather and sundry neighbours, alarmcd by my yells, closed in to unhook me.

Among those who rushed to rescue me from the goat was

the town barber who lived near our house. He was good with animals and, though his business kept him busy, he always took out a field or two on the edge of the town in which to graze several cows. As a result of the attack by Johnny's animal the barber was very pleasant with me, even before my first visit to his shop in company with my great-grandfather. I thought it the most wonderful place I had ever seen, and enjoyed every minute of my stay there.

The mirrors in the shop delighted me, as did the mixture of sweet and sharp perfumes from the coloured bottles on the shelves. I studied the battery of bone-handled razors above the wash basins and the picture showing an oily haired man with his moustache ends waxed out to the sharpness of needles. While I waited my turn the barber dealt with a big fisherman, his hair tousled, his blue jersey, trousers and high boots covered with silvery herring scales. The barber worked up a large mug of white suds and brushed these on to the man's face with the same kind of round brush I had seen my great-grandfather use at home when he shaved. The barber next rubbed in the soap, not looking at the man's face but out through the big window of the saloon. He talked most of the time but only my grandfather talked back, for the fisherman had to keep his mouth closed to prevent the barber's fingers slipping in.

I was amazed at the speed with which the barber sharpened a razor on the strap that was hooked on to the bench. He stroked, turned and flipped the blade back and forth so quickly that I could hardly follow it. The steel made a whistling sound as the barber drew it down the fisherman's cheeks leaving a clean track in the white soap. He did the same on the other cheek and then worked round the chin and under the man's throat. I could not keep my eyes off the razor at this stage for I was afraid that the man would bend his neck or the barber's hand would slip. He was not satisfied with his work for he brushed on more soap and went over the cheeks and throat a second time. When he had sponged the man and wiped his cheeks with a towel the fisherman's face was as clean and shiny as a pink bowl.

Then it was my turn. The barber lifted me up to the arm of the big chair and put a large blue towel around me, tucking it into my blouse neck. My grandfather told the barber what my mother had told him before he left home, that I was not to be docked. I did not know what this meant but when I asked her later I was told it meant cutting the hair the way some people did it at home with their own clippers. There were two ways of docking. The first was the easier, for the father ran the clippers over the child's head cutting off all the hair very close except for a fringe in front. The second was to cut the hair close from the neck up to the height of the ear and to leave the rest of the head covered thickly. This style was sometimes called the 'bowl dock' because it looked as if the home cutter had covered the top of the head with a bowl and cut round it. The barber must have listened well to my great-grandfather's instructions for my mother was well pleased with the haircut when we went home.

I was interested in everything the barber did but the speed with which he opened and closed his scissors, even when he was not cutting hair, amazed me. I did not understand how he could use scissors and comb without cutting somebody's scalp. I could hardly wait to get home to try to imitate him, but neither then, nor since, have I been able to achieve the speed or rhythm I admired so much on my first visit to the barber's.

That experience, and the fact that my father was what was

called a Navy man, combined to lead to disappointment and loss of temper in our home. My father had spent a full life at sea, first in the naval service and then in the merchant navy, which he preferred to the more regimented branch. Between the wars he ranged the world in the big Cunarders and White Star liners that were so popular before the advent of world wide air travel. He was away for long periods but assuredly his trips home on leave were occasions of delight. When he was away there were postcards from foreign parts and these always ended up in my hands. Though at first I could not read, I liked to look at the coloured pictures of water and buildings and mountains. Later, on looking over my store, I could make out names like Vesuvius, Danzig, New York, and St Mark's, Venice. This last was a great favourite because it was encrusted with fine silvery grains that glittered in the light of the oil lamp.

My father's bags were a treasure trove, for he always brought things we did not see at home. Among those I remember were a real silk scarf from Japan, two delicate fans from Spain, a square of lace from Malta and boxes of sugary fruit from North Africa. These were not always opened at once and I spent time looking at the palm trees, camels and people painted on the box lids. Like my great-grandfather, my father was a keen pipeman. He always brought a gift of navy tobacco, the real leaf, rolled up tightly by the sailors themselves into a shape like a long ice cream cone and bound neatly with ring after ring of thin brown rope from the sharp end to the wider end. I loved the sound of the big pen knife as thin slices were taken off to be rubbed and put in the pouches.

It is to my father that I owe an aversion to smoking that has lasted me to this day. Though not at home on land where, in the manner for mariners, he paced restlessly for most of his time ashore, he would take me for walks on Mountain Road where, at the top of the brae, he puffed contentedly, looking down on the sea. On one such walk I kept at him to let me take his pipe and though he tried to put me off, I knew that if I asked him long enough he would let me have a try. The results were predictable, as were the recriminations at what had happened to the 'poor child'. Also, while he was in no way to blame for the disaster that occurred when I tried to emulate the barber, it was one of his gifts from a foreign part that prompted the attempt.

He had brought, from the Mediterranean, two lovely miniature armchairs made of polished wood and hand-woven straw in a variety of colours. There was, I thought, nothing like it in the town and my brother and I just sat in them to be happy. Having learned from the barber how to snip, scissor and use the comb, and having an ideal chair in which to perform a hair-cutting operation, I smuggled the tools of the trade into our front room parlour. I wanted to surprise my mother with the results of the work I was about to do on my brother's hair, so far untouched by professional hands. His crop of fair curls was easy to do. While I was not able to snip-snip with the speed of a real barber, I was quick enough, and the curls fell on the floor all round the chair. The customer said nothing so seemed to be pleased too. Having finished to my satisfaction I conducted my brother into the kitchen, displaying him with pride. I could not understand why mother should have been so upset, and so unfair as to give me several painful slaps round the legs. While I was getting out of her way I heard her talking about my brother's hair being destroyed, mentioned shear-marks, a word I had not heard before.

She was even crosser a short time afterwards when I brought home a large armful of flowers. Along with several other boys with whom I played in the market square I sometimes ventured up the quiet Mountain Road. We never went much farther than the end of the long high wall between the church and the road. Behind the wall, between road and church, was a wood of high trees in which flocks of rooks were for ever cawing. Beside the rookery was another piece of ground called the cemetery. We had never seen into it because the wall was much too high for us to climb. We could not even see it from the field side for the bottom of the field was guarded by a very thick thorn hedge.

Sometimes our group of boys was joined by a girl, a little older than ourselves. I remember that we nearly always took orders from her and she took charge of some of our adventures. She could also climb better than most of us. One bright day she pushed and squeezed her way through the thick fence and into the field, from where she encouraged us to follow, and pulled us through the hole she had made when we got stuck. She said she had heard voices behind the cemetery wall and wanted to see what they were doing in there. We followed her up the field to a part of the wall that had more cracks and holes in it and where it might be easier to climb to the top and look over. She was on top long before we were ready to claw our way up. She encouraged us by saying that everybody was gone but that it was lovely inside.

When we were able to sit beside her and take in the scene we had no dread or awe. On the contrary, the neat place with its straight paths and rows of polished stones held and delighted us. We were particularly pleased with one large patch not far from the wall. It was covered, every inch of it, with flowers, in rings and squares and crosses, flowers of all colours. The girl said that it was a shame to leave all those lovely flowers there to wither and die, that she was sure our mothers would love to have them. Her words made sense to us. While she sat on top of the wall directing operations we dropped down and bore several of the nicest bunches to her. Then she helped us up and, carrying our floral treasures, headed for home.

My mother got the first offering. Her reaction was beyond all understanding. I received several of the limited number of thumps she ever gave me, and was hurt by her lack of appreciation. She herded the whole lot of us back up Mountain Road to the source of our treasure. Having seen that we replaced the flowers she scattered our band speedily. I was hustled home to sit in the house until bedtime even though the sun was splitting the trees and I could hear my friends laughing and playing in the square.

2

The School on the Hill

I remember school clearly from the first day, when I was conducted nearly a mile to the head of the town to be enrolled at Dunavan Infants'. Its name derived from the Gaelic, meaning the 'fort of the women', and the outlines of the ancient Celtic fort, or earthen fortifications, could still be seen in the field opposite the school. It was strategically placed on the brow of a steep incline running down to little Aughrim river, rising a few miles away in the hill of the same name and flowing through the town to the beach north of the harbour. The stream below our school and the small island it formed when it forked and joined again lent spice to our days, weeks and years of play. While providing an ideal after-school play territory the more restive of our company found it a temptation and a source of pain if the Pipes of Pan called too insistently during the school hours and the teachers found out.

Our three town schools were 'Primaries' but were known in the educational framework of the day as 'National Schools'. Kilmorey National was only fifty yards from my home but was for Church of Ireland children. The Presbyterian school was less than half a mile away from Kilmorey and was known as the 'Meeting School'. They all taught the same subjects to the same level and were controlled from Dublin. Compared with schools today they were hopelessly inadequate in every respect, except in the dedication and ability of their staffs. Teachers were required to handle three or four classes at a time with little equipment and a shortage of books. In fact the text books available as well as the stationery depended on the ability of the pupils to pay for nearly everything required. Thus, at a time when hard cash was short, and free books and equipment were unheard of, as much as possible was handed from generation to generation.

Nevertheless, from the first day I set foot in 'The Infants' until I moved on after completing the Second Class course, I thought the place a fairyland, and the next best spot to home. It was the pictures on the walls, the ball frames on which we counted, the plasticine with the perfume I had never smelled before, the coloured balls of wool swung so enthusiastically in our action songs, the wonderful harmonium that kept us in time when we strayed wildly.

Our female companions of the Infants parted with us when we went our different ways to the Boys' and Girls' schools. Integration of the sexes was, like integration of the creeds, avoided where possible.

The boys' school, with its bigger people and more crowded classes, was a disappointment. There was not much time for our individual requests and woes, nor much scope for doing the things we really liked when the mood took us. In time I found my feet and have many pleasant memories of the man known to everybody as The Master. I was told at home that he had come to our district when very young and that he spoke differently from us because he was from Cork. It was a long time until I was able to point that place out, first go, on the map.

Our school drew its pupils from as far away as three miles from the town and it was easy to distinguish the 'Town Ones' from the 'Country Ones'. The latter nearly all wore caps and were well and heavily booted. Low cut shoes were at the time rarely seen, even among grown-ups. It was hard enough to keep feet dry in boots what with the mud, and the pools of water on the roads. Boots were soled, and heeled, shod repeatedly and patched to keep them together as long as possible. There were many shoemakers in the town and townlands who could ensure a new lease of life for working boots by taking off the last of the soles, trimming the uppers and tacking on one-piece wooden soles and heels. Their work was called 'clogging'.

Good boots were also essential in the regular football matches, Town against Country, that were fought (and that is the right word) in our stony school yard. There was no need to pick sides for the factions came together automatically. The ball was of minor importance, and was not a real ball at all. The charging and dunching and kicking left little time for the niceties of ball control, even if these would have served to deal with the small canvas bag stuffed with straw and paper, and donated by one of our classmates whose father was a shoemaker. It was not even necessary to be in at the kick-off to take part in the game. If, having finished your piece, you tired of looking down the banks and decided to join in and lend a boot, all you had to remember was to make sure you kicked in the right direction.

One memorable summer we were able to buy a real leather ball by using a tactic sometimes forced on even adult teams in the district. Starting with the Master, we went round the houses with a note-book and pencil, collecting small sums from those able and willing to subscribe. The boy then given the honour of keeping her (our footballs were always feminine) brought bother on himself and his household, for any or all of the joint owners could and did call at all hours when the football fever struck, to demand the use of the ball. If, for some minor reason such as the completion of a home exercise or going to the country for a can of buttermilk, the custodian was unable to join the group, his worry that he would never see her again was intense.

It was during play hour (really a half hour) that the identities of town boys and country boys could easily be spotted, because of the make-up of their packages of bread, or 'pieces'. It was a fact of life at the time that some children had no bread at all. Those town boys who had pieces usually had a couple of cuts of baker's loaf while the country boys had home baked soda farls, of either wheaten or white flour. Sometimes their mothers gave them farls of what was called 'golden drop' meal, which was a finely ground maize. The bread was inviting to both eye and palate and was particularly appetizing when topped with butter and golden syrup. Exchanges of pieces were sometimes made at playhour for the country boys coveted the loaf of the town boys, who in turn tucked in to the wheaten and golden drop farls.

No matter what the weather our school had no heat between Easter and October. When the coal fire season did come round the school could be very cosy and friendly, especially when snow or rainstorms kept many pupils at home. The big open grate was well banked up with glowing coal and the Master allowed us to pull the heavy pine form close enough to rest our feet on the granite ground. If he was in a particularly good mood on such a day I thought it perfect if he read extracts from books he brought from his own home. It was close to the school fire that I first met Ivanhoe, the Artful Dodger, and Old Scrooge, and revelled in the magical happenings set out in Old Celtic Romances. From the latter we got enough to provide material for many a 'down the banks' adventure.

The Master would have been less than human if he had remained constantly unharassed and even tempered. He had much to contend with, not the least of his worries being the very bad attendance of many of the boys. The farms in our district are small, if fruitful, and could always be worked on a family basis so that there was never much hiring of outside farm labourers. It was little wonder that at seedtime and harvest country boys were kept away from school to help. Inclement weather too took its toll for some of the boys had a long way to travel, and only one mode of making the journey to school – on foot.

A good many of the town boys came from the homes of labourers and fishermen. Even when work was available wages were lamentably low. There were no state benefits of any kind for the unemployed. The fishermen were at the mercy of the elements and of the buyers who, at the time and for too long afterwards, were not overly generous with the prices they offered for catches. There was a limit to the quantity of fish that could be salted down for home use, or hawked round the country district. The result was that it was 'take-it-or-leave-it' for the herring men. Even ten years after my school days herring fishermen were forced to dump their catches in the bay to save the work and heartache of letting them go at prices as low as half a crown for a mease (about 52 dozen).

Some boys drifted away from school long before they were fourteen and some boys I knew at school were cooking between decks in tossing herring luggers out of southern Irish ports on the edge of the Atlantic before they were legally entitled to leave Dunavan. Substantial numbers of children were also not seen at school for the weeks during the blackberrying season, for precious shillings could be earned by picking the brambles clean and selling buckets of fruit to local dealers who set it off to dye works.

The potato-picking season played even greater havoc with school work and many boys did not put a foot over the school step for five or six weeks in the autumn. The picking of the crop was a long, laborious and cold job. To ensure that every single potato was recovered the method known as 'clatting' was used: after the drills had been opened, the pickers literally clawed, or clatted, the tubers from the soil. Many boys returned to school with hacked, teak-hard hands, and wearing new heavy boots they had earned through their hard work and absence from school. In the manner of veterans these hard men regaled us, gathered round their feet in the playground, with tales of the potato fields. Their boasts about the purchase and use of whole packets of Woodbines, at two pence for five, raised the lads in our estimation.

They knew every potato-picking house in the district and the ratings accorded to these depended more on the food that they served to workers than on whether or not the pay was at the standard rate of one shilling a day, or a top grade one-and-sixpence. One shilling a day and your 'mate' (meat) could be excellent or low grade according to what was given for the midday meal. If this consisted of cabbage and bacon with potatoes, or meaty Irish stew with tea to follow, or a plate of rice, it was considered very good, especially if the woman of the house did not send too much plain bread and jam to the field for the tea. If the pickers got herring on more than one day a week the word got out, and the herring houses had difficulty in getting experienced pickers.

We had outbreaks of mitching from time to time among boys who, losing the taste of school or unable to keep up with the work, felt lost. They took days off when the call of the outdoors became irresistible, and sometimes the urge to take time off struck the most reliable of boys, becoming so strong that the fear of parental or pedagogic wrath was forgotten in the glorious freedom of the banks of Aughrim stream, in dangling legs over the edge of the quay, or watching the shipwrights at work in the boatyard. Even the occasional long absence from the classroom was risked for the thrill of being free, briefly, while the others were hard at it.

The Master was not easily outwitted, however, as was illustrated when one of my desk-mates was charmed away. He found the first real sun of the spring on the big windows, the calling of foraging gulls following a ploughman in a field near the stream too much to bear. Throwing caution to the winds he raised his hand for permission to leave the room. The Master, supervising us hawkishly as we wrote a composition, nodded curtly and the boy left. The Master had a very strict rule about leaving the room. There was to be no dallying, the twenty yards from the door to the convenience being covered on the run. It was built into the wall at the top of the river slope, and climbing on top of the wall for long looks at the distant hills was forbidden. In particular there was to be no fraternising with the gentlemen of leisure who occasionally used the slope behind the school for taking it easy and sunning themselves while we, the hope of the future, were incarcerated. My friend, a biddable, timid boy who seldom incurred the Master's wrath, was out far too long. My concern seemed to convey itself to all corners of the room. I knew from the Master's face that his impatience was mounting. After nearly a quarter of an hour a lad in the front, not wishing to precipitate a crisis but in desperation, raised his hand in an unspoken appeal.

'The board, boy, the board,' the Master spoke grimly.

We all turned to look at the small slotted board beside the door. It clearly showed that the absent boy had, on leaving the room, pushed the sliding panel to the right, covering the printed word 'IN' and uncovering the word 'OUT'. Another five minutes passed. When the latch was depressed as softly as if a butterfly had landed on it and the door opened with scarcely a creak all heads were already turned and the tardy one was the target of all eyes.

Transfixed, he came no farther than the threshold.

'You have been out twenty minutes, boy.'

'Yes sir.'

'Why?'

'Please sir, I went down the banks.'

'Why?' It came again like a second arrow in the same wound.

'Please sir, I was talking to somebody.'

'I have told you repeatedly not to climb the wall and not to talk to anybody.'

'Yes sir.'

'And who, pray, were you talking to?'

'Please sir, Willie.'

We all knew Willie, who spent most of his life on the river slope and whom the Master considered a menace to rules and regulations. He absent-mindedly yet purposefully lifted the cane from the table at his side and spoke severely.

'You know that I have warned you about staying out too long

and especially about wasting your time with Willie. Can you give me one good reason why you have disobeyed me?'

The victim stared straight ahead and then grasping at a straw blurted out: 'Please sir, I have no sense.'

A hush fell on the room. Then the simple brilliance of the words struck most of us. There was a gasp, a titter and then open laughter. The boy was on the point of tears. We turned to look at the Master. He was bent forward, laughing too.

When he gathered himself he cracked the table with the cane bringing silence in a second.

'Sit down boy, sit down. You'll be the death of me.'

He was not always so easily softened. One particular incident involved three tough lads who took six of the best when the urge for freedom was too strong, and the sky cloudless over Slieve Binnian. They planned to take three days off in July, in the hope that the Master would have lost all track of their absence by the time the summer holidays were over in August.

Kilmorey and the Meeting always closed just before the Twelfth of July, the anniversary of the victory of King William over King James at the Battle of the Boyne in 1690. Our school always closed after the 'Twelfth' so that our holidays should include the Feast of the Assumption of Mary on the fifteenth of August.

It galled our prospective mitchers, therefore, that their Protestant friends should be off school while they were at work and they decided to have the best of both worlds. Moreover, not content with having the day off, they arranged to enhance the pleasure by playing near enough to the school to see the rest of us confined. To that end they chose a big field about a quarter of a mile from the school as the crow flies, the property of an eminent farmer, Bible scholar and lay preacher, who was said to bestow Biblical names, such as 'Bethel', 'Zion' and 'Heaven' on his fields.

The day passed and soon our holidays came, and went. We were back in school after the 'Fifteenth' but it was late September before there was any inkling that the Master even suspected there had been mitching in July. Anyway, all of us, including the three culprits, were far too busy trying to memorise the list of Latin roots the Master had written on the board to bother about past escapades.

The studious silence was broken suddenly as he rapped out:

'Come up here Matthew, Jim and Pat.'

After some whispering and nodding the three boys mentioned rose, along with a second Pat.

'Not you,' said the Master, pointing at him. Relieved, the boy sat down.

I am sure that nobody, least of all the boys named, had any idea why they were asked to come forward. We thought they were to be interviewed about their compositions. When they were ranged before him he illustrated the fact that he had a keen eye, a long memory and the ability to keep a rod in pickle for as long as required.

His first question was harmless enough.

'What is today's date?'

The chorus came: 'The fifth of September, sir.'

'Exactly,' he said. 'And what were you three rascals up to playing marbles on the headrig of Johnny's "Heaven" on the Twelfth of July?'

There was no adequate answer. The malingerers took what was coming to them in the knowledge that once again they had underrated the Master.

While we knew he was a stickler for good order and instant obedience, there were many things about him that we liked. We knew he could vault a wall that we had to climb, and do standing jumps a foot farther than any of the senior boys. Though married with children at Dunavan school, he was light of foot, and nearly always when coming out after play-hour to marshal us into school he was on his toes, lifting his heels as he jogged, clapping his hands.

He urged us to try our abilities at long and high jumping, as well as throwing the weight. He prepared a two-stone weight with a short loop of rope round its bar so that we could swing it backwards and forwards between our legs, throwing for distance and height. Besides his own example books were cleverly used to provide us with inspiration and heroes. I remember hearing for the first time of Matt the Thresher, whose hammer-throwing inspired us to many efforts, when the Master read us a passage from Charles Kickham's *Knocknagow*.

Similarly, we first learned of the joy of running as hares and hounds when he read us the account of the paper-chase in *Tom Brown's Schooldays*. When he let us loose to imitate the boys of Rugby School the loanings and paths by our little river had never seemed so attractive. He also introduced handball to the district, providing shutters for the back windows of the school, and encouraged both ourselves and the local men to use the school yard as an alley.

During my final years at the school, I achieved a measure of importance because my father, on leave after one of his trips sailing the world, brought me a set of boxing gloves, a gift not appreciated by my mother, who was more than willing to let me bring them to school. They were, as far as we knew, the only boxing gloves in the district. The Master taught those of us who displayed an interest in the art of self-defence the basics of boxing, both in guarding ourselves and in gentle assault on opponents.

As usual in most schools there were a few boys who, because of their toughness and unscrupulousness in schoolyard fights, struck terror into boys who were not able, or inclined to fight. We had one boy from Glasgow who, having come to live with uncles in town, was widely feared among us. We did not know it then, but the Master was well aware of the situation and always supervised the little schoolyard glove-bouts that took place at play-time, insisting on the observance of the rules of boxing. It became evident that a couple of our quieter boys made a very good shape, while our Glasgow terror held aloof from the Marquis of Queensberry nonsense. Trapped, however, through boasting, into a schoolyard contest with the gloves, he was soon a pricked balloon: with no kicking, butting or elbowing allowed he was lost. It seemed that the comparative peace that descended on our stony schoolyard was a direct result of my gift gloves, cleverly utilised by the psychologist at the helm.

The Master also excelled in the teaching of singing and then, as now, the children of the district had good voices. He chose his songs from Robbie Burns, Thomas Moore and the Petrie collection, and would regularly ask boys to sing for the class ballads they had learned at home. He had no instrument but, starting us off with the tuning fork, he backed us and kept us right, building up a repertoire of unison and two-part songs. No songs since have matched those that told of the Glories of Brian the Brave, Bonnie Charlie, brave Bruce and gallant Wallace. The lovely melodies, catching something of the beauties of Avoca, Bonnie Doon, the Last Rose of Summer, and Eileen Aroon are still with us.

Though jealous of our out-of-school reputation, the Master put no curb on our after-hours recreation, even if we returned to the school to play, and we regularly went to the river bank below the schoolyard, scarcely believing that anybody had such a nice recreation ground. It was in the pools that formed along the stream that we learned to swim, later increasing our skill on the safe beaches bordering the harbour. We had a theory that if we learned to swim well in fresh water we would swim higher on reaching the salt water because of its buoyancy. Not all of us had bathing suits or even rudimentary trunks each time the notion of a dip struck us, though that did not bother us unduly. Having posted a lookout on the high side of the stream we took a chance, and had our uninhibited naturist colony on the secluded stretch of water. Often enough our lookout deserted his post and almost before we knew it was disporting himself in the pool with us.

The athletic promptings of the Master inspired us to a form of jumping unique to our school. We had dozens of jumps along the stream that, hopefully, took us from bank to bank. Some were narrow, and entailed jumping from the high to the low side. They became progressively harder and for those of us who were nervous or who had soft feet, the leaps and landings attempted by some of our barefooted classmates were scaresome. There were regular drenchings as boys overrated their powers in the acceptance of challenge. It was quite common to see one in a state of undress, drying out shirt and trousers over a crackling brushwood fire before venturing home to face parental scolding or worse.

One of our more adventurous jumpers introduced a new method of clearing the stream. He cut and peeled a nine foot pole and used it to vault the water. The new idea caught on and soon we could all make a reasonable good shape at the vaults.

Following on the skirts or our group we sometimes had a big innocent fellow four years older than ourselves. We knew he was not too bright but liked him. One lovely day, just made for jumping, with the blossoms snowy on the sloes, he made it clear to us that he would do any jump we did. He insisted on borrowing our pole, removed his coat, rolled up his trousers and sleeves, spat on his hands and charged, pole extended at the water. Five yards from the edge of the bank his confidence ebbed, rather dropped like dough through a hoop. Unable to stop he shouted despairingly:

'Oh! I'm drown-ded.'

Making no attempt to spring, he ran knee-deep into the middle of the stream. It was in no spirit of cruelty that we fell about laughing. Gamely he tried again, several times, running in and twice throwing himself down to avoid that fate. We recovered our pole and showed off to our hearts' content, while Jimmy glowered. He grabbed the pole again and, moving well back from the water, shouted:

'I'm ready now.'

Closing his eyes he muttered like a Wimbledon finalist talking himself to victory, set course for the stream, placed his pole and took off. It was a winning effort if his nerve had held, but at the apex of the vault his arms went limp. With a despairing wail he slipped down the pole and sat down in mid-stream. We did not desert him but praised his fine attempt and gathered dry twigs to replenish the crackling fire until Jimmy's clothes were dry.

He was one of those boys in our town who had never been known to go to school. As far as I knew he could not read or write but, at a time when young people had never heard of pocket money, Jimmy always had a shilling or two. He was never short of Woodbines and, indeed, to attract our attention and maybe to impress us, he sometimes produced a short clay pipe, such as could be bought in the grocers' shops in the town. In spite of his lack of schooling he was an expert in the fish-hawking trade. We heard he was an orphan. His father, who seemed to me to be very old, owned a donkey and cart, and went to the harbour to buy herring and mackerel, but it was usually Jimmy who went round the houses with the fish. He got the name of being very tight to deal with, and well able for the stingiest countryman. Certainly, though he was a poor river-jumper, he could handle his 'yoke' (as he called his donkey and cart) to perfection, particularly when any of our boys were about, when he would pretend he did not see us and show off his skill with the reins.

Once, while sunning myself on Mountain Road with a tattered magazine, I saw Jimmy get himself into a fix and a battle of wills that was at first funny, and then sad, for his little animal refused to be a party to Jimmy's showing off. The pair of them approached smartly enough, the boy sitting on the shaft. He condescended to notice my presence though it was obvious he considered his custodianship of the donkey placed him a notch above me. As the yoke neared the entry leading into a wide yard he pulled on his right hand rein, calling loudly what sounded like, 'Houl aff!'

If it was an order neither the donkey nor I understood it. The strength of the pull on the rein forced the shaggy head to the side so it appeared that Jimmy intended to turn the donkey's head out into the middle of the road and to aim the short back shafts at the entry. The animal stopped, its legs braced. Jimmy swung himself to the ground. He reached into the back of the cart and picked up a stick, moved to the donkey's head and pulled, or tried to pull it forward, and right. I am not sure but I think the animal closed its eyes, and kept them closed for a few seconds. Jimmy's next move was to push as hard as he could against the shaft, attempting to force the animal and cart into position. But the donkey was adamant. He did not move an inch. I winced as the boy struck it on the flank, shouting:

'Will you do what I tell you, you brute?'

There was no sign that he was getting through. He raised his stick to strike it again when a woman passing with a loaf of bread called out:

'Stop that, you cruel rascal.'

The boy weighed her up and going round to the other side of the cart dashed up to the animal's head and began to tug at the reins, breathing hard. The donkey yielded grudgingly and the cart came round with the back pointing to the entry. With an air of triumph Jimmy stood in front of his beast, caught the winkers in both hands and should, 'Back! Back!'

He was wasting his breath for the donkey held hard. Pushing and shoving, entreating, threatening, he tried to impose his will. It was useless. Then, almost on the point of tears, he jumped up and down and, half crying, shouted:

'Will you do what I tell you, you donkey, or I'll knock your brains out!'

The beast had opted out and was not hearing at all. A couple of friends had joined me to watch the struggle and we were clearly on the donkey's side. So was the woman, who reappeared and moved up to the street fountain to draw water. She looked on with an air of patience which belied her inner fury.

In a whinging tone the boy addressed his charge:

'You'll not conquer me. I'm telling you that. You'll never conquer me.'

The woman asked:

'What are you trying to do, you silly fool?'

'Are you blind? I'm trying to back him into the yard.'

'Well, he's not going to back for you. If you had as much sense as he has you would front him into it, lead him in. I'm telling you if you hit him again I'll throw this bucket of water about you.'

Light, and discretion, slowly filtered in. Unwilling to yield, but conscious that she was on the right track, he led the donkey past the entry, made a U-turn and led it back again. With no trouble at all from the animal he made his turn into the yard. The cuddy had opened its eyes now, and seemed happy enough with the manoeuvre.

3

The River

Today I could walk the whole length of our river, from the harbour to the steep bank at old Dunavan, and never see a sprickley, eel, trout, or a jenny wren's nest. Yet before we had reached our teens we knew every rock where the tiny fish hid, and each overhanging shelf along the river bank where the cunning eels lurked. We did not bother much about frogspawn or tadpoles but were always on the look-out for sprickleys, which we put in glass jars and displayed proudly in our homes.

The 'spricks' fell into three classes: the thin, rather plain, brown kind; the fatter, matronly-looking fish known to us as the 'bog'; and the choicest of the three, the one with the red breast we called the 'robin'. With trousers rolled high and with heads bent close to the water we paced up the stream carefully, lifting stones and herding, with cupped hands, any spricks that darted away before us. We worked in pairs guiding the little fish to the shallow, shingly side of the stream and so into our jars. We were not rough and cruel with the little beauties: though they did not live long in the jars that was no fault of ours, for we changed the water regularly and dropped in crumbed bread and titbits of river weed to feed them.

Our attitude to eels was different. In our eyes they were wicked predators and deserving of summary justice. For that reason we armed ourselves with short, straight ash twigs with mackerel hooks corded to them. We stalked the enemy to their lairs in crevices under the broo and if, when the water was agitated the eels slid out we 'clepped' them, for the home-made gaff was called a 'clep'. In spite of the dislike we had for the slippery fish, we firmly believed it had curative powers in the easing of sprains. One boy in our company, who spent the whole summer barefoot, regularly had an eel skin round his ankle or wrist 'to cure the strain', he said. Perhaps, in the manner of all huntsmen, he got great satisfaction out of displaying trophies of the chase. He was very proud of his skill with the clep, and adept at peeling the fish, nicking the skin round the base of the head and, with a steady pull, removing the sheath of skin in one piece.

One summer we became friendly with a man who, to our amazement, was willing to pay, in pence, for all the eels we could bring him, for he liked them fried. This was unbelievable, for in our opinion eels were hardly worth catching, never mind eating. Our champion clepper explained the whole thing adequately by saying that the strange customer for eels was an Englishman, and he may have been, for his accent was not Irish. He remained in his four-wheeled caravan in our square for over a week, stabling his horse in a yard across the street. When we climbed the steps to look over his half door we saw him sitting at his stove, or frying eels in bacon fat. Whatever the taste, the smell was mouth-watering but in spite of that we never chanced bringing our eels home to ask that they be fried for tea.

We found out that the stranger sold articles of drapery round the town and country. He was an unusual member of the tribe of packmen or peddlers that we saw often walking the roads. They all carried packs of goods wrapped in oil cloth. They sold bolts of tape, reels of thread, needles, thimbles, scissors, cotton and flannellette materials for dressmaking. Usually they arrived in the town in the long cars that carried passengers and papers from the nearest railway stations. There was nothing trampish or beggarly about them and during their stay in the town they lodged in local houses that made meals for people and put them up for the night. Some that I saw were very foreign looking, with beards, and though they could speak very fluently and seldom left the door without selling something, they had curious accents. It was generally thought that they were Jews. One of them who came to our district several times a year sold watches and gold and silver trinkets from his pack.

Our busiest and happiest days along the stream were between April and October, for it was then that the sprickleys were running, the hawthorn bushes heavy with perfume, the big crab apple tree that leant over the water giving pink promise of loads of fruit to come. When it did ripen we climbed dangerously into the leaning branches and picked it to eat, bring home for jelly or, as a last resort, to use for ammunition.

We loved birdnesting and took pride in listing, but not showing to our friends, the nests we had found in the forks of hawthorn, crab and ash. 'I have a thrush's, a yellow yorney's and two jinty wrans',' was a proud boast, countered at once with claims to a whin checker's and a moss cheeper's at the foot of Mulligan's field.

Not all our band were interested in just spotting the nests and keeping the locations secret. There was the odd vandal who, in spite of us, would handle the eggs, taking a couple to blow them, although he knew perfectly well that, devoted and all as were the parent birds, the mere touching of the eggs meant that the nests would be forsaken. There was among us boys who were so angry at such conduct that they would face up to the destroyers and resort to fisticuffs to defend the nests.

Eddie, one of our best birdnesters, and a real lover of birds, took me to a slender ash, a field's length from the stream, to show me a thrush's nest only he knew. He cautioned me to approach softly or I would frighten her off. From below we could see her beak and tail over the edge of the nest but she stuck tight as we stood beside the trunk. We kept our secret and came back regularly until one day, when the parents were absent, he climbed up and reported delightedly that there were five skinnies at home. Eddie allowed me to join him to watch the miracle and sure enough the pets were gaping and crowding in the cup of wool and grass.

The next day they were still in residence, but jostling for room. The following day we saw on our arrival that one of them was well up on the edge of the nest. As we watched he jumped, or was pushed, into the world. With no help at all from his rudimentary wings he zig-zagged to the ground. Eddie tenderly lifted him from the grass and, keeping him in the hollow of his hand, shinned up to the nest to replace the winded but still lively skinny, watching while he made room for himself. We hoped that all would be well and could hardly wait to return to check, only to find that two pets were on terra firma.

Eddie was distracted, not knowing what to do to keep the brood intact until they had wings and tails wide enough to keep them aloft. He devised a plan, saying very sensibly that since the nest seemed too small and the side walls too low to keep the skinnies in place, it might be a good idea to raise the wall all round to make escape and fall more difficult. He plaited a rough collar of dry grass to fit round the rim of the nest and, climbing up, set it in place, ensuring that it would remain where it was by pushing small twigs through it into the nest edge.

While so engaged he was subjected to a good deal of verbal abuse from the parent birds. Finishing the work he stood at the bottom of the tree, looking up, and said:

'If they want to get out of that they'll have to fly and if they get into bother it's their own lookout.'

We never saw them stranded again, and in a short time the nest was empty.

It was only a short distance from the thrush's nest that I participated in an operation so sophisticated that it could only have been set in motion by a stranger in our midst, someone foreign to our town. Only occasionally did we have contact with boys from the outside world. For most of us the area beyond the hamlet of Ballymartin, two miles away on the coast road, was as big a mystery as Timbuctu, a place that took our fancy when we were pointing out features on the ragged school map of the world. The parish church a couple of miles away on the other road round the coast was the limit of the territory we ranged. Belfast was only a name to us and we knew nothing about the life of its people or what we would be likely to see there. Boys and girls from outside our district were so admired that they were given a place of honour in our company and play. Sometimes we had coastguards at the station above the harbour who hailed from England. The son of one of these came to our school for a short time. He was a confident boy but I had to listen hard to what he said for I could not make out half of it. I heard that he was a Cockney. That went some way to explaining the accent but it was some time before I understood what the term meant. He must have had difficulty following our idioms and our speech, heavily tinged as they were with Scottish overtones.

A well remembered visitor, one beautiful summer, was a lad who came from Belfast to stay with his family in a holiday home. He immediately became a big man among us. His singing Belfast accent intrigued us. He made it abundantly clear that it was a privilege for us to be allowed to chum with him. I knew it was, for me, because I was only on the fringe of the group and the big boy was a few years older. He wore a big tweed cap with newspaper stuffed in behind the peak to raise the front and he tilted it at a rakish angle. We, who never wore caps if we could possibly get out of it, nevertheless admired the city boy's style. I gathered that he lived near the shipyard and that his family had something to do with building the big liners. When he held court by the edge of our stream or on the beach we listened enthralled to his stories of the men who worked at 'The Island'. All of them had nicknames, but for all we knew about their way of life they might as well have been natives of the Solomon Islands.

It may have been his wish to stress his superiority or his desire to call attention to his imaginary manhood that prompted him, one day, to make us sit up, saying:

'It's time I had a shave.'

We looked closely at his gingery face, but could see nothing to justify his assertion. He was softly downy but that was the most that could be said. He explained that he could not perform the operation in his own house for his father was up from the city and would kick up, especially since he intended, as he said in terms that would never have occurred to us, 'to use the oul' fellow's blade'. We listened intently as he told us how he could lay his hands on some soap, a brush and the cut-throat razor. He graciously signified that if any of us wanted to join him while he took off the beard he would not mind and bade us rendezvous at the cattle pound on Mountain Road next day after lunch.

Not even Jim Hawkins waiting for *Hispaniola* to clear Bristol on the first stage of the voyage to 'Treasure Island' was as eager as I was for zero hour. We hung about waiting for him to emerge from his house. He stepped out casually but winked at his assembled retainers, tapped a bulging pocket and signalled us to head up round the corner towards the river. He chose the arch of the river bridge as a suitably secluded place. There was water available but he insisted on having hot water for he did not intend to pull the chin off himself so the beard would have to be softened. We lit a small fire of twigs and nearly burned the fingers off ourselves handling the enamel mug. His mother would never use it again because it was soon so discoloured that he tossed it into the stream after shaving.

None of us liked the look of the razor he produced.

'I can shave myself,' he said, 'but if any of you fellows want to have a go at it I'm game. It'll be practice for you.'

I, along with all the boys but one, wanted nothing to do with wielding the blade. A senior member of our band who would, if challenged, have had a go at taking the hair off Samson, volunteered. Since my first visit to the barber's I had always wanted to try my hand at stropping a razor and had gone through the motions of rubbing and flicking a table knife on a flat board at home. I asked to be allowed to have a try on a real strap. Bill hooked his father's lovely bit of leather on a twig stump and showed me how it should be done, working slowly. He was not too deft for he nicked the strap a few times. My attempts were even more disastrous and the leather was in a mess by the time I was finished. He airily dismissed my mistakes and lay back against the grassy fence to have his face soaped, brushed and rubbed.

The razor man stood by and at a signal from the director began his delicate task. Fortunately he made good in higher educational circles in later life for his attempts to shave the Belfast boy did not augur well for a career in barbering. Most of us watching intently winced as little bits of skin were removed along with the down. The terrifying business was over at last with no complaints from the victim. One of our band had in his pocket a tattered copy of last week's *Marvel.* The scraps of porous paper served to staunch the leakages in the sitter's face. His jaws were like a ludo-board by the time all the patches were in place. He rose higher than ever in our estimation when, after an interval, the patches were eased off and his face was cleaned up. He ran his hand over his face and said:

'That's better. That'll do me for a week.'

Then, coming back to earth he looked round at the tools and ordered: 'Throw that strap in the river. If the oul fellow sees it he'll murder me.'

We were never very sure of the outcome of the matter or if his father found out just what had happened to his shaving gear. We thought that there might have been trouble for when we called for the city boy next day his father was curt with us and told us to go away and not bother him. We thought we saw him looking out from behind the curtains of the front bedroom.

On Monday the two of them left for Belfast. As they rounded the corner of the street the boy winked at us with the eye farthest away from his father and stroked his chin, which had healed by that time.

4

Sea Legs

While, in our heedless years, we had neither the depth nor the time to know much about such things as social deprivation, slavish work, injustice and downright need, we could not fail to know that the majority in our town and district had not much money. Even among those who were reasonably comfortable, regular allowances of pocket money for adolescents were exceptional and, for school children, undreamt of. Most of us were happy to be given or to earn a few pennies for little jobs we did. Anyway, the small amounts of spending money sufficed to satisfy our need for the occasional handful of sweets or one of the weekly magazines such as *Penny Popular*, *Boys' Own*, *Marvel* or *Gem*. If we were ever flush and could run to a threepenny *Buffalo Bill* we had not only provided ourselves with hours of delight but had in hand valuable bartering material that could be used to draw on the penny dreadful resources of the class mates. The pulp publications balanced a reading diet that was supplied mainly from the limited number of school text-books, with a helping from the sombrely bound and too-adult books we found on the shelves of our elders. There was no library in the town but there was an active lending system among friends and neighbours that ensured the rotation of books.

I still remember the lovely wife of one of our district's schoolmasters who, on occasion, walked with me as I trotted home after serving my daily stint as altar boy at our parish church, two miles from town. We served for a week at a time and then had a couple of weeks off. She talked to me of school and books and offered to lend me what I wanted from her store. So began a period of pleasure and profit for me. She lent me, a volume at a time, every book in her family encyclopaedia. I found this a wonderland and, though much of it was far beyond me, I revelled in both word and picture.

We saw that the people who lived close to our coastline were always on the lookout for anything that could be used to increase or conserve, their supply of hard cash. Though fishing was the main source of money and food some women, children and even men foraged at the sea's edge when the rocks were uncovered. The driftwood they collected provided many a good fire in the coastal cottages.

When tides ebbed far the uncovered rocks yielded buckets and sacks of winkles, called 'williks', as well as two edible seaweeds, dulse and slock. The latter two were brought home, well washed, and prepared for sale. The dulse that dried out in ribbons was extremely salty and particularly appetising for inlanders. Slock (and I have not seen it eaten for a long time) came off the rocks as a dark green, slippery and very sandy weed. It required much washing before being boiled and reduced to a blackish jelly, a kind of 'noir-mange'. My memories of it do not induce a flow of gastric juices but it was prized by those who thought it tasty and good for them. The young doctor was a customer for the sea food when the old lady who went round selling it out of her basket called with him. Fried with bacon it was said to be appetising.

Williks were scarcely ever eaten in our district because the people did not like the look of them and because when they were boiled to make it easier to extract the worm-like inmates of the shells the yield was not worth the trouble. Yet over the years there was a steady demand for the shell fish from London where, to the astonishment of local pickers, they are considered a delicacy.

When long lines and skiffs were yielding few profits our small boat owners ranged the bay and the shore for 'crubean' (crabs) and lobsters. They sowed their creels, made of wooden rectangular bases, bent osier rods and tarry twine, and hauled them regularly. Lobsters were too profitable for home consumption but crabs supplied tasty side dishes in the cottages. Both crabs and lobsters were caught or hooked at rocky places along the shore and Leestone beach was an excellent territory for the crustaceans.

It was here on a sunny day, after I had bathed myself to exhaustion, that I joined a lobster man of my acquaintance. I saw him in the distance peering and stooping among the weeded rocks and, because I liked talking to him, I made my way round the pools to the edge of the sea. He never went to sea now, yet had served many years in the windjammers and luggers and he could not keep away from the water. He wore high leather boots, a blue jersey and the blue peaked cap favoured by many fishermen at that time. He was a good talker and free with his answers to my queries. Indeed he seemed to be pleased to have somebody to talk to who would show interest in his sea lore.

He said he had a dozen creels off the harbour but he enjoyed a bit of crab and lobster hunting among the rocks. He knew the best rocks, the best lairs to which the creatures returned again and again. He had caught some real big ones on the shore in his time, lobsters that would not have been able to get through the tunnel in a normal lobster creel. I thought he was making it up when he told me that he had caught one a couple of years ago 'that long', and he parted his palms to a distance of about two feet. He must have sensed my doubts for he invited me to call at his cottage any time I liked and he would show me the front claws that he had varnished and glued to a board.

It was not long before I presented myself at his home for a look at the remains of the monster. If anything he had been underpraising his prize. While I was there he took a carpenter's ruler and showed me that from claw socket to tip each mandible was thirteen and a half inches and four inches across at its broadest.

As we talked on the shore he went about his immediate task of trying to cleek the lobster or crab that, he was sure, was under the big rock. He went on commenting, half to himself and half to me. The creature he was after was personified and, regardless of its sex, he kept referring to it as 'he'.

'I cleeked them here before. It's like an eviction. Pull him out and as sure as there's a bill on a crow, another one will take his place. I've cleeked them out of this hole as long as I mind.'

'How do you cook him?' I asked, dropping into his style.

'Either lobster or crab,' said he, 'there's only one way to cook him right. Drop him right away into boiling water.' I winced, but he went on: 'It has to be done, and it's fairer to him than starting him in the cold and bringing him to the boil. Do you know that he shells? Every June it happens. That's how he gets bigger. Off comes his coat and he's kind of soft and black and sleeky. But by the time July comes he's as hard as ever.'

'But how does he shell himself?'

'I'm not sure, but he's able for it. I've seen him without his shell and I've seen whole shells on the bottom, but I never saw him at it. They tell me he comes out backways. If I get one in here I'll show you his broad tail with a kind of hinge on it. They'll tell you he's stupid going into a creel without knowing how he's going to get out, but there's nothing stupid about the way he shells, now is there?'

The lobster man seemed glad that I shared his high opinion of his friend and quarry. In truth, ever since that long past chat I could never bring myself to take any part in the trapping or eating of either crabs or lobsters. Like all boys of my day I became a keen line fisherman from the end of our big pier, yet I had too much regard for the durability and intelligence of both lobsters and crabs to cook them, however humanely.

As our skill in the water grew we did our swimming and diving in two deep freshwater pools nearer to the coast than the little island below our school. One of them was on the Kilkeel river before it joined the Aughrim at O'Brien's pool, near the harbour. The former, when there was no drought, was five feet deep at most, six yards across, and called 'The Battery'. Years before, water had been taken from the river at this point to supply water power for the boatyard on the harbour bank near Leestone beach and a wooden aqueduct led the river water from the Battery to turn a large wheel at the yard. O'Brien's pool was at the junction of our two streams and was deeper and wider than the Battery. Beside it was a pleasant green where we frequently played football and our version of cricket.

The ultimate in river dipping was enjoyed at the mouth of the river. At full tide the seawater pushed well up the narrow estuary, widening our bathing place. Best of all was that, in our half salt pool, sea wrack and long ribbons of kelp had established themselves in patches so that when we took deep breaths and dived we had no trouble in imagining that we were 'Coral Islanders' looking for pearls in underwater caves.

The river-mouth pool had another attraction for us because it was the last resting place of a famous old schooner, *Dunburve*, that had years ago foundered in a north-easterly snorter and been driven ashore at the river mouth. When we kept our eyes open underwater in our dives from bank to bank we could see the barnacled timbers and conjure up exciting images.

The harbour then was only half the present size but the numbers of trading craft that came and went were far in excess of today. While a few battered steam coasters used the port, most of the traders were sailing schooners and ketches that were always busy making passages to Lancashire, the Clyde, Belfast, North and South Wales, as well as London. Some of the craft were owned by Mourne coal and hardware merchants and some operated by local owner-skippers who traded with cross-Channel ports, fetching and carrying whatever freight could be picked up on the fringes of the Irish Sea, and the west coast. All the coal, timber and most of the flour we required came by schooner and Bangor blue slates, used extensively on farm houses, came from North Wales in the sailing vessels.

Then, as now, a main plank in our economy was the fishing fleet on which many of us had relations working. Most of the herring luggers were 'unengined', though in my schooldays engines were being installed, giving our sea harvesters a wider range of operations and a greater margin of safety. As well as the bigger craft there were dozens of twelve to twenty foot open boats called 'skiffs'. Few of them were motor powered but gradually old motor car engines were used to drive small propeller shafts. The skiffs were family owned, and worked and earned their money at inshore fishing for herring in autumn, long line fishing throughout the year, and in sowing lobster and crubean (crab) pots in the bay. When long line fishing, they carried crews of six and seven. Men used strong lines of great length barbed with dozens of hooks to catch mackerel, whiting, cod, coalfish, and ling.

Far more important, as far as we were concerned, were the cockle-shell craft, called punts, that were tied up round our harbour. They had no masts but were rowed with two light oars. More often than not they were sculled, using a feathering stroke, by a single oar in a stern rowlock. Some of the schooners towed, or carried, punts on their trips but at any given time there were always a few of the little boats moored to the bollards, or 'pawls' as we called them, set on the quaysides.

Just as we took a chance to steal rides on bicycles left by countrymen along Mountain Road we purloined punts to make glorious trips round the harbour waters and among the schooners tied up in the old basin. All we needed was one small sculling oar and a knowledgeable fisher lad to skipper the craft. If, unluckily, the punt owner happened on the scene while we were making ready to push off it was just as easy to scull out to mid-water as to return to the steps or the iron ladder and risk his tarry palm on our ears or sea boot on our backsides. When the sun was sparkling on the bay and there was not a trace of broken water, we delighted to round the big pier and scull out to open up Kilkeel beach, with the red brick Coastguard Station perched above it, and to see the sweet contour of the Mournes from

Donard to Finlieve.

We thoroughly enjoyed our line fishing for blockan and mackerel from the pier and we had one type of angling, or rather 'snagging' fishing, that required a good eye and speed of hand, called 'jigging for fluke'. When the tide was flowing, with the water crystal clear at a depth of four or five feet we used a special hand line with a dozen hooks affixed at distances of five or six inches. The hooks were unbaited and were drawn down to the sandy bottom by a lead sinker. There they lay while the fluke, perfectly camouflaged, slid in over the sand with the tide. Through the clear water we watched until we judged that the fish were over our hooks, and then we jerked, or 'jigged', the line swiftly. If the lucidity of the water was right and our reactions good we were often successful in adding a flat fish or two to our catches.

Though our pier fishing absorbed us for hours it was nothing compared with fishing out of punts in the bay. The 'coalies' and blue mackerel were bigger out there and hungry for our bait of salt herring. On calm days just looking down into the depths at the patches of sand and the gently waving seaweed whangs was nearly as good as pulling in a fish. When, in midsummer, the beach below the Coastguard station was dotted with family parties, we loved to show off by edging our punt close to shore, even beaching her if there were no breakers. From our berth a dozen fathoms out we could dive from the gunwales and swim to our hearts' content.

Sometimes when the herring luggers were hove-to a mile offshore, waiting for the tide to berth, we circled the lazily rocking craft where there was not a sound, the crews making up for lost sleep during the previous night's labours. Once a tousled head appeared out of the fo'c'sle hatch as we drew near. The cook was shaking a leg and making tea for sleepy-eyed men. He asked us aboard and we scrambled up on the deck, hot under our bare feet. We thought we had never tasted anything like the strong tea with condensed milk, and the thick slices of bread and butter were just the thing for our hungry crew. It never occurred to us that we were foolish to venture a mile or more from shore on punt excursions. The sun on the sea, the gentle breeze and the zooming, banking gulls made nonsense of any hint of danger.

One perfect day conditions were just right for acceptance of a challenge by two tough 'Shore Road' boys to race to a metal buoy marking a sunken wreck two miles south-east of the harbour mouth. Our rivals, not much older than we, were skilled water-men and had already found their sea legs in nights at sea with the luggers. Their punt was not as low in the water as ours, with its six man complement, and they sculled expertly, taking turns, so that by the time they reached the buoy they were thirty yards ahead of us. As we approached, a jerseyed boy in the winning punt stood on the prow and shouted his victory cry. The buoy, seen close, was rusty red, pear shaped, and anchored to the wreck by means of a chain. The narrow end rose six or seven feet clear of the water and the buoy rocked gently in the almost imperceptible swell.

The lad leaped and caught the top ring, lapping his bare legs as far as he could round the metal pear. He clung tightly repeating his victory shout while his shipmate stood off a couple of fathoms' length. We hove-to, disappointed at our defeat. Then the buoy began to tile, ever so slowly, as the lad's weight pulled it off centre. The ring came over until he was dipped to the hips. He kicked wildly, achieving nothing but a recovery by the metal marker that, having tilted to one side, did the same thing to the other, with malice of forethought it seemed to me. It settled into a slow rock and roll, and each time it came off the upright the boy went deeper and got wetter. We were now hooting with laughter and derision as he abandoned all pretence of not being annoyed, even scared, and he called for help. His shipmate brought the punt in close to try to catch him on the dip, but in the end the swaying boy had to let go and splash and struggle to haul himself aboard.

He seemed to think that we were in some way to blame for his humiliating experience, and threats and promises came across the sunny water. We rowed away, leaving him 'in his pelt', to us a Mourne phrase. His jersey, shirt and pants were spread out in the little boat and would soon dry in the light breeze. The drenching did not do him the slightest harm but was accepted as an essential part of the hardening process that would turn him into a seaman, able to take his place aboard any ship, anywhere. His annoyance was caused mainly because his humiliation had been witnessed by what he considered to be a crew of landlubbers.

He and his shipmate completed full lives at sea, in the Royal Navy and aboard big tramp steamers that range the seven seas between Helsinki and Auckland, Yokohama and Belfast. Even those of us who were not destined to spend our lives at sea found our sea legs around the harbour on summer days, or as youthful guests on overnight fishing trips with the fleet. We knew everybody around the harbour, for in the years before the War it was a very small place. When half a dozen trading schooners were at home and the fishing luggers and skiffs were docked, there was scarcely a free berth or a bollard without its mooring lines.

Around the start of the War it was decided to build a new breakwater to form a pincers with our pier, to make the entry safer when the wind was from the north east, and to provide a stretch of sheltered water inside the harbour area. Our main interest in the breakwater was that it provided a sheltered lagoon where we could swim within bounds. As we improved in the water the new pier presented us with a challenge. To swim the thirty yards between the piers and back again, all the time in deep water, proved we were well past the learning stage. Though I did not admit it, my first there-and-back swim was terrifying. The outward trip was bad enough but the return leg, after a delay on the breakwater to muster courage, was worse, especially since the long smooth swell from the bay was exerting its power in mid-passage. The new structure and its low supporting blocks of concrete on the slack water side was an ideal place for young swimmers and divers to check their progress. Claims to be able to swim two blocks, three blocks and so on were flung about in school. To be able to swim from the tip of the breakwater to the beach gave a boy high standing.

We heard with surprise that some of the old fishermen had never learned to swim. One bearded veteran who frequently smoked his pipe at the pierhead did not like to see us diving off the top or venturing into deep water. In chatting with him one day when I was drying myself after an hour of diving and swimming he told me that he had never been in the water in his life except the time he fell into Newry canal and they had to pull him out with a boathook. He hinted that this unwanted dip had been brought about by something he had drunk. In all our swimming in the harbour we never had a tragedy, though one incident on the harbour beach could have had serious consequences.

Along with two older boys from my school I was dressing on the beach after a dip. I was pulling my shirt over my head and my companions were nearly dressed. A school friend of my age, barefooted and tarry from helping his father at a nearby skiff, trotted smartly down to the edge of the water. With amazing speed he dropped his pants, whipped on tattered trunks, removed his shirt, and edged along the narrow ledge to the first concrete block. Then he was at the second, then the third and, looking back at us as if to say, 'This is easy', reached the fourth.

Here he stood, looking down into the calm water, stretched himself and slowly, in the manner of an Olympic springboard man, brought his hands above his head. We knew that the water below him was at least seven feet deep and that unless Hughie had improved his swimming, it was no place for him to be taking a header. He dived, if the belly flop could be called a dive, and went under. The water settled briefly. Then there was a commotion, a lashing and foaming as he came to the surface. From where I sat on the warm pebbles I could see the surprise and fear on his face before he went under again. On reappearing he was unashamedly terrified for he knew now that there was no bottom nearer than two and a half feet. His choking shouts were loud enough for someone twice his size and we could make out clearly the words: 'Oh! Ma, ma!'

I was petrified, for I knew I could do nothing in the circumstances. My bigger companions, nearly dressed, showed no sign of leaving the shingle. When Hughie went down again the older boy dashed to the ledge, sidefooted along it and when level with our drowning friend, flipped out a towel that somehow or other the lad grabbed. He was hauled in until the big boy was able to grasp him by the hair and haul him up on the concrete block. So tightly did the frightened, bedraggled Hughie hold on to his saviour's legs that he nearly brought both of them into the water. If Hughie was quick in divesting himself of his clothing, he was a laser beam itself in getting back into his trousers and shirt. Teeth chattering and fear still in his face, he shot up the beach and headed for home.

The provision of an inner dock to provide more room for the fleet was a wartime concept too, and made a great difference to both fishing and schooner trading. An inland basin was scooped out, the sides piled, and an encircling road laid down. I vaguely remember gangs of men shovelling soil and clay into bogies that were dragged by horses on a narrow gauge track for dumping away from the new basin area.

Much clearer than the men and the activity during the making of the new dock is the memory of an ancient mariner who caused laughter, among the common folk anyway, on the day of the official opening of the dock. We boys were not interested in the prosperity they said the new facility would bring, nor in the dignitaries who had come to our town to make speeches on the big occasion. The function provided us with yet another opportunity to dash round among the groups of people on the quay and to enjoy our freedom to the utmost.

On the big day we saw the fishing boat that was to make the official entry to the dock berthed down the channel near the pier. She had several flags on her masts, and the well-dressed men aboard were the important people who had been invited to the opening. The programme had not taken into account the life-long daily itinerary of one of our oldest and most experienced seamen. He and all his forbears had been rowing and sailing the bay all their lives, in cockle-shell dinghies and skiffs. He ranged the waters between Derryogue and Crubean Point nearly every day, and nobody knew better than he the best spots for mackerel and coalfish. It was rarely that he returned empty-handed from his lobster creels, though sometimes he cast no line and hauled no creel: he just rowed, thinking long sea-thoughts.

If anyone told him that because the dock was to be opened that day, a temporary restriction had been placed on the movement of boats he either did not believe it or pooh-poohed the whole idea. It was his harbour and he was coming home after hours of solitary happiness away from land. So it was, as we waited for the lugger and officials thought over their speeches, the little punt shot up the basin, past the Windy Gap, with the bearded man bending and opening his shoulders to shoot his craft into the new dock, the first to do so. Many saw the joke, though the resounding cheers must have puzzled the old man as much as they delighted the majority of the onlookers.

Most of our fishermen, however, were friendly men who seldom turned down boys' requests for a place in a skiff or lugger, provided parental permission was forthcoming. So it was that we went on short trips to the bay with the lobster men or on skiffs that fished for herring just off the shore at spawning time in the autumn.

My mother dreaded the sea for her father had been lost in the bay, within sight of the shore, when she was a girl. The long-liner *Twin Sisters* with a crew of six, had been swamped in a fierce squall and sank with all hands. Hence my requests for permission to have a night with the herring skiffs was turned down repeatedly. She consented at last, however, and allowed me to go out on a calm evening in an open boat with three crew men. The skipper was a young but experienced man who had seen much service in the bigger boats. Along with him he had two other men who were equally competent.

Though the September day was bright and mild the skipper advised me to bring a warm coat and muffler as well as a 'piece'. He said it got cold in the bay as midnight approached, and I was sure to be hungry before we reached home again. Our skiff, a twenty footer, had a foremast with a big brown sail furled away, but ready if we needed it. We had a small engine housed aft in front of the skipper who controlled it as well as the tiller. The engine, from an old car, had been adapted to drive a propeller shaft and gave us a speed of about six knots. A mountain of brown nets was piled amidships and I sat on top as we cleared the harbour mouth. A dozen boats were motoring ahead of us with a bevy of small craft following as we reached the bay. All were soon ranging up and down, some heading north east and some in the direction of the lough mouth looking for signs that would point to the presence of herring shoals. During our prospecting we could see the fading line of the shore and Big Binnian clouding down for the night.

Darkness came rapidly but the skipper, having studied the workings of the seabirds, had decided to shoot his nets about a mile and a half off Derryogue cove. We could see the home lights on the foothills, and around us were the masthead lights of the *Maid of Mourne*, *Evening Star*, *Kindly Light*, *Coleen Bawn*, and a score of fleetmates. The nets were meant to hang upright in the water, in the swim path of the herring. To this end one edge of the train was lined with corks and, at longer intervals, large inflated, tarred floats called pallets. The other edge of the net was weighed down with blue kidney stones from the beach, tied on with short lengths of thin rope. Having decided to shoot, the skipper put his engine to 'slow ahead' and helped his men to pay out the net over the stern.

When the last pallets and stones had slapped and splashed over the quarter and the soft darkness was thick around us, we ate our bread. After a short time of rocking gently, steadied by our train of nets stretching a quarter of a mile into the night, I did not need the satisfied comments of my colleagues to tell me that something good was happening. The sea sounds were muted but there were birds working and there were little splashings astern of us. Our skiff dipped and rose and dipped again deeper. The skipper decided to haul. The men bent and strained at the net. It soon became clear that we were loaded. There was agitation in the net and much flapping and jumping among the snared herring. I saw for myself that, as fish came aboard, there was glinting silver all around. The sea off our quarter was winking and gleaming with phosphorescence. The men were chuckling with delight as they hauled, although they were soaked and arm weary, with only a third of the train abroad. At first they shook each fathom of net as it came in to loose the fish, but then they stopped this, leaving net and herring to pile up. Soon all the space between the engine casing and the bow was filled above the gunwale and we were low in the water.

We heard a skiff come close between us and the shore. A voice hailed:

'Any luck Frank?'

'Aye! We're loaded. How about you?'

'We have hardly a tail.'

'We can't take them all. Will you give us a hand?'

'Certainly. Wait till I work round astern of you.'

He did this quickly and skilfully in the darkness, found the tail of our net and, receiving permission, began to haul by the light of a bobbing hurricane lamp. After an hour of heaving and straining he had come close to us and was as well loaded as we were with some of the train still in the water. Regretfully both skippers decided to cut away, leaving a part of our net to drift and sink with its herring. The two laden skiffs, humped like sampans, kept close as they crept over the still water. As we rounded the pier we could see figures leaning over the iron rail and heard the old familiar cry:

'What luck?'

'About thirty maze.'

I swelled with pride and sensed that the watchers on the pier rejoiced with us. I was dead with sleep, for it was after midnight, but felt part of a tight little group when Frank said:

'You'll come out with us again, son?'

Felix, as superstitious as the rest of our fishermen, put in:

'Aye, do. You'll be very welcome. You're good luck.'

5

Carts and Cargoes

I made my way home in darkness up the steep bank past McKeever's cottage. Except for the glimmer of oil lamps in some of the Shore Road houses where wives waited to welcome their husbands home from sea, it was pitch black, for we had no street lighting. I swung my fry of prime herring on a piece of thin rope threaded through their gills.

Though tired next morning latent excitement woke me early and I was on my way to the scene of last night's triumph at nine o'clock. It was Saturday so there was no school and I was free to spend the whole day at the shore. The place was busy, for there had been good catches in most of the skiffs. The boats had to be emptied early so that the local hawkers could complete their rounds before dark and the cadgers with their horse-drawn carts, from outside the district, could head for home.

I returned to our boat and found my shipmates finishing the shaking of the nets. Their oilskin dockers and high boots were thickly scaled. Their fish had already been sold. It remained for them to count the catch into wicker baskets and hand-hoist these to the quayside above by means of a slender swinging derrick rigged to the mast. It was then the custom to reckon the catches in mease (maze). Kneeling in the wall of the boat two men counted their herring, throwing in three fish at a time. Each throw was a cast, and it took two hundred and eight cast and one herring, that is fifty two dozen and one, to make a mease. They called the tally in sing-song voices – ending thus:

'Seven and thirty, eight and thirty, nine and thirty, forty, a cast, a fish, and another.'

This completed what was known as a long hundred. Four more long hundreds were counted, making a total of a mease. If anything over ten shillings a mease was offered it was considered good. Prices were often much less. I was proud of my boat, for with thirty-two mease we had earned twenty pounds for the night's work.

Herring were dumped into the barrows and baskets of the hawkers and the wooden boxes on the light flat carts of the buyers, sometimes from as far away as Tyrone. Hurrying from the harbour the hawkers walked the town streets and the country roads selling their wares at two and three pence a dozen. The walking basket-men earned their money, for their country tramps took them for a dozen miles by the foothills for a profit of maybe three or four shillings.

It was usual for households to lay in a mease or half a mease of autumn herring salted down in glazed crocks, for use with floury potatoes and home-churned buttermilk during the winter. So it was that most houses with open fires had, among its cooking utensils, a grid iron on which the herring were cooked, after steeping overnight.

The greater part of the catches was bought for export by local merchants. The fish slid from the baskets on to long box tables in front of girls known as 'gutters', wearing heavy aprons and headscarves. With incredible speed they flicked their knives, disembowelling the fish and flipping them over their shoulders into wooden barrels. As the level of the fish rose in each barrel, men shook shovels of coarse salt on the layers. Finally the lid was tapped into place, the last hoop hammered on, and the barrel wheeled back ready for carting.

The autumn herring trade brought gutting girls to our little town from the west Donegal coast and sometimes our workers went to Scotland to handle the herring there; and often enough our herring buyers employed coopers, barrel makers, during the season.

All the heavy barrels of brined fish were carted out of the district by our own men who hauled a ton at a time, or ten barrels, fourteen miles to one or other of the railway stations. They were paid one shilling and sixpence a barrel. Some consignments were carted the five miles to Greencastle on the Lough shore, opposite the packet station of Greenore. A paddle steamer linked Greencastle pier with Greenore, connecting with the nightly steamer that carried passengers, mail, livestock and cargo to Holyhead, and so to London, on the old London and North Western Railway. Thus the herring I had, according to a shipmate, 'lucked' into our skiff would be delivered in a French Channel port or a herring-loving village in Belgium or the Netherlands.

The fish carters were an important part of our horse-and-cart transport system on which our connection with the outside world depended. Everything we had to sell outside the area had to be sent by schooner or by horse and cart, and what we needed came in by the same means. The full time carters faced long journeys winter and summer for, as well as transporting fish, they brought loads of flax to the linen mills, and pigs, lambs and calves to neighbouring market towns.

Our grocers depended on the carters to keep up their stocks

of essential foodstuffs. A recent privileged look at the freight account book of a well known carter showed entries as:

10 bags sugar
5 bags flour
10 cwts bran
$^1/_2$ cwt paper
1 bale tobacco
4$^1/_2$ cwt bacon
1 drum oil

Exotic items he carried as the Christmas season approached were:

$^1/_2$ cwt sweets
$^1/_4$ cwt cloves
$^1/_2$ cwt ground ginger
2 casks baking soda
2 cases currants
2 bags rice
$^1/_2$ cwt raisins
3 cases oranges

He also carried six cwts of lozenges, perhaps as a measure of the prevalence of coughs. It is likely, though, that the consignment was assorted, and that among the cough-easers were those that were sometimes used by inarticulate suitors to convey their feelings. They were known as 'conversation lozenges'.

Our crossbred farm-horses were of a smaller type than the stronger animals that undertook the long hauls with heavy loads to and from the railway stations. Bigger farms kept two horses for ploughing and harvesting, but smaller farmers doubled up, working with neighbours on farm tasks. As many farmers, especially those who lived in the foothills, were skilled stone dressers they used their farm-horses and strong carts to bring their finished granite products to the harbours of Kilkeel and Annalong for shipment.

It was only just prior to the Second World War that the shipping of granite square sets and kerbing (called 'shodies' and 'cribben'), for paving the dockland streets of cross-Channel ports, was discontinued. None of our local streets was tarred during my schooldays. All the paving granite was raised and dressed on the mountain slopes in shelters fashioned of loose granite boulders or in lean-to sheds at the mountain houses. The stone dressers carted their products the long miles to the coast. When the stone carts, emerging from Mountain Road, faced our stiff town brae on their way to the harbour we stopped our play to lend vocal and sometimes practical assistance.

Local merchants bought the paving stone and brought in the sailing schooners that put out regularly from the Mourne shore with their heavy cargoes. The stonemen were paid in cash but sometimes when the merchant had a shop, payment was made in kind, in the form of groceries, cheese, bacon and flour. The famous fleet of Mourne schooners was our lifeline, for it brought in all our coal and took out our potatoes and granite. There were several coal merchants in the town but no deliveries were made; the town dwellers collected their own bags of fuel at the stores in little handcarts, bogies or trucks borrowed from the shopkeepers or merchants.

Many of us at school had relatives serving in the fishing

boats or trading schooners. Two quiet boys who flanked me in one or our big scarred school-desks were the sons of schooner captains. My second cousin's father was a noted hard-driving owner-captain. So we were free to step aboard and have the run of several schooners while they were docked and taking aboard granite, after clearing their holds of coal. We could climb down to the decks of the herring luggers nearly anytime, but the schooners were more interesting, with roomy spaces and nooks where boys could hid and play; and when sudden rain squalls swept in from the bay and rocked the sailing ships in the old basin we felt snug and safe below decks, in the fo'c'sle, with the small mid-floor stove nearly red hot.

We were able to walk the timber decks of *Mary Grace*, *Trial*, *Guild Mayor*, *Phyllis*, *William Shepherd*, *Volant* and *Alpha*, to carry water from the iron fountain on the quay, and do odd jobs for the skippers; and daringly we climbed a little way up the rope rungs of the mainmast riggings that soared steeply to the cross trees. Some of the monkeys in our company were natural born climbers. Several were destined to sail in the windjammers, to mount the riggings in earnest, to furl topsails in roaring winds, while cross trees swung and creaked wildly against the low dark sky.

Many of the schooner skippers were oldish men and most that I remember were bearded, tight, trim, and spare framed, their blue caps, with shiny peaks, set squarely on their heads. The owner-captains were businessmen as well as mariners, picking up cargoes where and when they could, doing their own brokerage work and making speedy passages in the severest weather between port and port all round Ireland, and to docks along the Irish Sea.

It was a measure of the importance of schooners and luggers in our lives that in our school drawing and crayoning exercises, and winter night work at home in the light of the oil lamps, we were always fond of showing the big windjammers in full sail or our luggers breasting the swells on their way to sea.

From listening to schooner boys and men I learned that life aboard ship could be hard. Though food was not normally skimped, it was plain to the point of monotony. Fresh bread, usually home-baked on the griddle, was taken on board before sailing from home, as well as a couple of buckets of herring and potatoes. Small quantities of tea, sugar, condensed milk and some butter were laid in, and occasionally flour and a bag of raisins were included in the stores. These ensured that 'sea duff', something special, could be dished up. Rock hard sea-biscuits formed emergency rations.

Cross-Channel runs could be done in a day or less if winds were fair. Far too frequently they took much longer and there were occasions when our schooners were forced to remain in distant ports by prolonged spells of bad weather. At such times, with no income, strict budgeting was necessary. Schooner skippers had to be good managers and the fact that many of them made money and built fine houses attests that their skill with figures was on a par with their seamanship.

As a result of their reputation as good seamen, and their deep knowledge of coastal waters, local merchants put valuable schooners in their charge. The crews were paid on the basis of freight carried and the owner's profits were directly linked with regular sailings so that, in bad seasons, returns for all concerned were pitifully small.

Some of the boys at our schools had their eyes on berths in

the boats and displayed their abilities aboard ship at a very early age. In the evenings they would go aboard, always on the lookout for the odd job, washing down decks, brushing holds, pumping bilges or doing errands for skippers who were usually very fair in remunerating their youthful helpers.

I recall one youth who, though living on the edge of the country and well used to helping his father with horses and cattle, was irresistibly drawn to the sea. He seemed destined to spend his life on it, and his tilt with a schooner skipper was, to our band of boys, both pleasing and memorable. He could climb riggings in seconds, sit astride cross-trees, walk side-footed from the lovely figurehead of a schooner to the tip of a graceful bowsprit projecting over the water. He was happiest when on deck or nipping along the gunwale of a schooner, and he was always picking up a shilling or two from skippers who made use of his willingness and agility.

One day when we were playing, climbing and hiding around a stack of tree trunks awaiting shipment at the old basin, we saw the sea-mad youth engaged in an argument with a skipper. The young fellow was putting up a good show but the man, intolerant of insubordination, had driven him ashore and waved him away.

We closed in on the furious lad who showed us a shilling that the so-and-so had given him for a half-day's work in the cold. He felt like firing it back, accused the skipper of being capable of wrestling a ghost for a ha'penny and he stated his determination to get his revenge. This he did skilfully and effectively. Knowing the downright dread all sailors have at omens of bad luck, the injured boy, having learned that a black cat had recently met with an untimely end near the river, hastened to the spot and returned with the stiff creature. Binding its legs together with a piece of rope he motioned us to conceal ourselves behind the pile of logs.

He reconnoitred the schooner, making sure his enemy was below decks. In a flash he was in the rigging, then astride the yardarm far above the deck. Not yet high enough he lapped his legs, like a convolvulus, round the varnished spar above and was soon level with the forepeak, the top of the mainmast, where he lashed his feline pennant.

His descent was even speedier than his climb. Safe on the quay he paused to admire what he had accomplished before yelling the skipper's name, leaving out the 'Mister' or 'Captain' to which the man was entitled. The man's peaked cap appeared above the hatch, and seeing the defiant boy he climbed the last few steps of the ladder to the deck. He ordered the boy sternly to get away from about him for he would take nothing of further abuse.

The lad stepped back and pointed aloft, dramatically, shouting:

'Good luck to you, Skipper.'

The latter came ashore to ascertain what exactly he meant. He was annoyed and worried but, bluffing, ordered the lad to remove the token of evil at once. Mocking laughter came from his foe. We joined in, from our timbered retreat. The argument was long and fierce while idling seamen, scarcely able to hide their smiles or sympathy, looked on. The upshot of it was that the captain grudgingly agreed to cough up one and sixpence to add to the original shilling, as the settlement due to his conqueror.

This was not an isolated dispute involving a skipper and a youthful casual labourer. Shortly afterwards another lad, this time as gentle and inoffensive a youth as ever aspired to a berth at sea, crossed swords with a schooner captain. It appeared that he had been given a thin sixpence for a series of tasks aboard a vessel. Looking ruefully at the coin, and then the captain, the lad kept his own counsel, for he knew that argument would be useless.

Surprisingly he said:

'Do you want me to make your tea, skipper?'

'Aye! Put on the teapot.'

'I'll have to go for water. The bucket's empty.'

'Away you go then, and then go home for I'm sure your ma has your tea waiting for you.'

The boy hopped up on the quay and then trotted in the direction of the water tap. Looking round carefully he ran to the slipway where he dipped his bucket in the oiliest, saltiest stretch of slack water he could see. The skipper stopped him putting any more tea in the pot than would make one mug, told him to cut one slice of bread, butter it and then hurry off home. When the tea was drawn the boy asked if he should pour it, did so and mounted the ladder. He did not leave until he was sure the skipper had enjoyed his first long draught of the liquid.

6

Away from Home

Our carters faced competition from a steam-powered monster that freighted in heavy goods once a week from the railway station. A huge steam engine with a wagon in two brought bricks, timber, cement, flour and the like for local suppliers. Our name for the giant was 'The Big Engine'. The name of one of the drivers is as clear in my mind as that of my schoolmaster. Phil Turley was the important man who guided his gleaming puffer along the coast road and eventually to the top of the long hill that descended steeply to the river bridge. He always brought it to rest in the little school square beside my home.

The machine could be heard long before it reached the brow of the hill. The roads had not yet had the benefit of Mr McAdam but were paved with roughly crushed stones from one of our foothill quarries. They were tamped down by steam roller and kept in place with a mixture of clay and mud we called 'clabber'.

In time the roads disintegrated under the pounding of the iron hooped carts and horseshoes. The occasional grinding by 'The Big Engine', and the rain, frost and snow soon broke them up, and potholes were numerous. In breezy, dry weather dust was everywhere. The roadmen, armed with barrows, shovels and big brushes made piles of dust along the streets and wheeled them away.

When Phil's engine crunched and clashed its way through the

town it never failed to attract us. We revelled in the deftness and skill of the driver and in the power of the machinery he controlled. We watched him manoeuvering his charge round the right angle corners, his hand rotating so speedily as he turned his gleaming brass steering wheel. At a touch from his finger the fly wheel slowed its revolutions to almost stop and then, as in a sudden fury, when he opened the throttle it spun with the speed of a dancer. The white steam hissed and the piston slid in and out greasily, beautifully. We could see the glow of the coal fire on Phil's oily coat. The big funnel puffed up black smoke with all the importance of an express train. When the engine was at rest and Phil was taking his ease we climbed into his cab and tried to emulate him, imagining ourselves masters of the monster. It provided us with a special thrill and a fright the day it ran amok.

Everything was normal as we pushed and jostled out of the school gate at hometime. We waited, for we heard Phil's engine coming up Doran's Hill and passing the first milestone out of the town. He covered the distance between us ponderously, slowing up as he reached the top of the descent to the town junction. We ran alongside calling a greeting, but Phil, though a friendly man, was like all good navigators not going to take his eye off the way ahead. He loosed a couple of fierce jets of steam and outdistanced us to the end of the workhouse wall.

It seemed to us, as we ran to try to keep up, that the engine and the wagon were going too fast. Half way down the hill this was very evident. Sensing that something was wrong we stopped. The juggernaut slipped and crunched and slithered on its way to the bottom of the incline. We had no idea what to expect but, when the destroyer passed the town end of the big wall and reached the first of the houses, it veered left. We saw Phil jumping clear and sprawling and rolling on the cobbled pavement. The runaway lurched further to the left and floundered thunderously into the parlour of the blacksmith's house. Dust and plaster few, glass smashed and tinkled. There was a sudden silence as, with a last puff and gasp, the engine expired.

Every door on the street was open as we reached the wreck. People ran out to see that had struck their street. Nobody explained to us what had caused the engine to bolt but we heard someone say that perhaps a coupling had snapped, affecting the steering, so that even Phil could do nothing to prevent disaster. For nearly a week afterwards we kept ourselves late for school stopping to look at the damaged house. We had never before seen such a sight for the whole front was open. A bed was balanced on the edge of the bedroom floor. We could see a wardrobe and chair against the back wall. Nobody had been hurt, for as was usual in our town the parlour was never used except on Sundays and special days. The blacksmith and his womenfolk had been working at the rear of the house, away from danger.

Far more frightening than even the runaway engine were runaway horses, especially if they were yoked to the stumpy stiff carts used by our farmers and stone carters. Scared, galloping horses on our narrow streets sent everybody running for safety. One such runaway brought out the courage and skill of a young man who was lounging at the street corner. We first knew that something exciting was happening when we heard the shouts of men and a woman's scream from the direction of the old post office. A driverless horse, dragging a bouncing cart, was speeding towards the hill. The reins were dragging the dusty ground, the horse's head was high, the eyes wild, and its path erratic as it charged the junction.

We scurried for safety to the top of the steps at the corner but the young man ran up the street close to the steps and then angled out to meet the crazed animal in the middle of the road. He turned and ran alongside the horse, stooping to grab the ragging reins. At the junction he threw all his weight back on the ropes, his boots sliding along the ground. The horse's head was jerked sharply to the side. Its shoes struck sparks from the stony road, its forelegs crossed and it plunged forward and down. One cart shaft ploughed the street and snapped, the jagged end close to the sliding man. There was a confusion of flying hooves, spinning wheels and leather harness, and a wild neighing from the floored animal. It made wild efforts to rise but the young man now standing over it promptly sat on his head, flattening it to the ground and rendering it helpless.

Regular trips were made to the town by light spring carts with high sides, known as the 'porter carts' because of what they brought in from Newry. Perhaps they carried other more potent and expensive beverages than the black liquid that was so much appreciated by droughty farmers and fishermen. They kept our dozen public houses well supplied.

I heard that the porter cart drivers were always willing to give a lift to any of our people who were walking at a distance from home. Indeed any of our carters, while travelling light, would willingly give a lift for the sake of the company and out of his goodness of heart. There were cases of young members of our local football teams missing the team brake (a large horse drawn carriage) on return trips from away games. It was said with confidence, 'Oh, they'll be home on Monday or Tuesday on the porter cart.'

Nobody needed to be stuck for transport into or out of the town if he had a shilling or two to pay the fare on the passenger-mail cars that ran twice a day to the railway stations. They worked up to the war years when they were edged out by small motor buses. The two-horse long cars had accommodation for five or six passengers on each side, their feet resting on steps and facing the hedges. In cold and wet weather the passengers were provided with waterproof blankets to cover their legs. The driver and his assistant sat on a double seat facing the front and drove two fine stalwart horses. The service was operated by a provincial firm, but managed by a local family. Even in the worst of weather when passengers stayed indoors the horse cars ran, for they had a Government contract to carry mail.

My one and only trip on a long car was made to the railway station at Warrenpoint to make connection with the Newry train. My naval father was indirectly responsible for the journey though he was away from home at the time. One of his gifts for my brother and me had been a pair of navy man suits complete in every detail and made of the same blue serge as the real thing. While we were very proud of the round caps with ships' names on the ribbons, white vests and lanyards, tight blouses with blue and white piped collars, it was the bell-mouthed trousers that intrigued us most. They gave us an advantage over any of the boys in our school classes for it was only when a boy left school and started to work that he was allowed to wear longs. Mothers were reluctant to allow their boys to dispense with the knickerbockers that were worn by schoolboys. Because of our unique new outfits my mother decided to make the trip to have photographs taken so that my father could have some.

The journey to the station by way of the lovely wood of Rostrevor and by the edge of the lough was memorable. We were not allowed to take up room on the side seats but were seated in the shallow compartment that ran up the middle of the car. To our delight it was known as 'the well'. We had never before seen a train and took in every detail of the wonderful conveyance. Even Phil Turley's 'Big Engine' could not compare with it.

Newry was wonderful, a big crowded place, with sights and sounds even better than we had in our town. The cathedral was very impressive, but the high point of our visit to Newry was the session in the photographer's. There was no trouble at all in getting us to smile, for the operations of the photographer ducking in and out of a black cloth, and his exhortations to watch the dicky bird reduced us to laughter. It needed sharp taps on the head from a wedding ring to settle us.

The return trip on the train was even better than the outward run for we knew what to look for. We were getting sleepy when we climbed into the well of the long car for the last leg of the trip. We had blankets over us and were most comfortable as we listened to the talk of the driver and his helper. They assisted passengers on and off the car, delivered parcels at houses along the road and, as darkness began to fall, whistled at gateways to let people know that the papers they had brought from the railway station were there for the picking-up. The lights of the oil lamps were on when we reached our town. Very tired we stumbled home from the Car Office before falling into bed and deep, lovely sleep.

Our eventful day in the big town provided us with much to think about and to discuss. The recollections of the ticket office, the porters, the flag-waving guard and the train whistle, as well as the performance of the people on the long car, gave us much material for acting-out. The photographer with his black cloth and dicky bird routine was a treasured memory for a long time. When the photographs arrived they were ample evidence that the little man knew his business and more were ordered. They were in our family album for years and always brought back a very special day away from home.

My longest stay away was at a house in what we called the country. It began at the fringe of fields just outside the town where the houses thinned out, where cows backed in under the hawthorns in winter, where in spring we saw the first black-faced lambs and where, in autumn we ventured up long, unfamiliar loanings to pick blackberries. The wide band of stone-fenced fields that stretched from the town's edge to the foothills and the blue range itself were a closed book to us. We were too busy in the town trying to find time for all the things we had to do to know much about rural ways and life in the real country.

The houses to which we walked weekly for tin cans of buttermilk, with real butter floating on the top, were not far out of town. Fields of the loveliest blue-blossomed flax had been pulled, retted, and scutched in the half dozen scutch-mills in the district we had a thriving flax market in the town.

Once, on our way across the fields for buttermilk, a friend and I came upon a brimming linthole. These were common in the district, along the courses of rivulets that formed drains by the margins of low-lying fields. Big rectangular hollows were scooped out and when the water filled them the green flax was packed in to soak and rot the hard skin of the stalks. After drying out on the field, the flax was ready for 'scutching', and the dry skin, or 'showes', was beaten off to leave a tough off-white fibre.

To our delight someone had left a large wooden tub floating on the miniature lake. It occurred to Tom that here we had the chance of a new experience. There was no reason why I, being the smaller, should not, under his watchful eye and steered by the long pole he pulled out of the hedge, enjoy a trip in the tub. If all went well he could profit from my experience and perhaps go farther and faster in the water. He helped me aboard, advised me to cross my legs, tailor fashion, and keep as low as possible, sitting very still. I was to keep a grip on the pole while he gently nudged me out from the bank.

His advice was good and all went well, but when I lost my grip on the pole, the tub, as though alive, began to rotate swiftly. I panicked and tried to steady the craft, but it tilted, dipped and dumped me in the linthole without warning. Though I must have been nearly five feet tall and the water only four feet deep things were made difficult by a thick layer of soft mud on the bottom, and I went in to the chin. I was so shocked that my wallowing attempts to swim did little to help me make a quick escape.

My companion, through fear that if I drowned he might be blamed for that lamentable outcome of a perfectly easy and safe manoeuvre, managed to reach me with his pole, somehow or other. I seized it and he dragged me to the bank, bedraggled, muddy and scared out of my wits. My mother got no buttermilk that week but I got a long evening and night in bed after a brisk tanning. If Tom's ears were not burning as a result of the recriminations that were heaped upon him in his absence his extra-sensory perceptions must have been on the dull side. It was a week before he reappeared near my home looking for the pleasure of my company.

A couple of chances came during my childhood to spend a

few days in the 'real' country. A family of school friends had a grandmother, uncles and an aunt who lived in a long, low farmhouse well up in the foothills. Permission was given for the stay and we were lifted to the heights in a long spring cart. We sat with our bundles, legs dangling over the tailboard of the cart. The trip up the country road, with their uncle singing 'When the fields are white with daisies I'll return', was a very pleasant experience.

It was harvest time and the main work was the reaping of the oat crop in three fields near the farmhouse. This was all done with scythes. Two uncles took regular spells at mowing but it was necessary to get the help of a neighbouring farm labourer if the crop was to be 'knocked down', as they said, while the good weather lasted.

This little man's skill with the scythe enthralled me. He did not rush his work but effortlessly, tirelessly, and cheerfully he swung his way across the gold and green field, swathe after uniform swathe. I heard for the first time the unique and satisfying sound of sharp steel in succulent stalks.

We all took turns to lift the corn but the thistles were too much for town hands and we turned to the easier stacking, or 'stooking'. The work was not interrupted by a return to the farm for the mid-day meal. Cans of tea, mugs, milk and a big basket of split griddle farls covered with butter were brought to us.

During my few days on the farm I was always hungry but plenty of boiled eggs, new bread and butter, milk, potatoes and porridge filled all gaps. Though I was fond of porridge, my mother's neat little saucepan of the stuff, dished up at breakfast time with carefully poured milk and a dusting of sugar would not have sufficed in face of the supper time hunger of field workers.

The routine of the porridge-making was most interesting. I was allowed to take my turn at the fan bellows by the side of the big open fire to keep a steady glow under the large black pot. This was suspended by means of a crook linked into a vertical bar on the crane, and it could be swung out over the hearthstone when the contents of the pot were ready.

The water was boiled, the salt shaken in, and the meal brought in a tin scoop from the meal ark in the corner of the kitchen. The meal was last year's, home grown, and ground in the mill with the water-wheel three miles away. As it was dusted in by hand the water was kept on the move with a large wooden stick, always in a clockwise direction. The porridge was ready when it was of even consistency and plumped and japped gently. It was pulled out, off the direct heat and allowed to cool.

One of the uncles, a big kindly man, asked his sister, the woman of the house, to let me have a turn at stirring the mixture. They always called it 'stirabout'. She agreed, first allowing me to dust in a little meal and then to use the stick. I believed him when he counselled me that I should always stir in the same direction or I 'would take the twist out of the stirabout'.

There were no niceties about disposing of the steaming porridge. The pot was placed on the granite hearth stone and each member of the family was given a bowl with either milk or buttermilk, and a spoon. We took what we wanted and there were seldom requests for seconds in the form of tea and bread.

As night closed in we liked to watch them milking the cows in the breath-warm byre. It was our job to hold the candle while the milk jetted and foamed into the big cans. We helped with the 'fothering up', filling the manger with sweet hay and held the hurricane lamps as the men tugged armfuls of fodder from the stack in the haggard.

Poultry clucked in the outhouse and settled for the night. The pair of dogs, still with us, were as tired as we were, but kept at our heels until bidden to their house. As the autumn night closed in we could see the scattered lights of the town and tried, a little longingly maybe, to spot our own. Out at sea the masthead lights of the inshore skiffs winked, scattered, and settled, as men made up their minds at what time to shoot their nets, and wait.

The country night sounds were conductive to sleep for youngsters who were already half asleep before they sank into deep, strange feather mattresses. The scrape of a branch on the window pane did nothing to stave off slumber, and the soft breathing of the wind in the big Scots pine at the gable was a fitting close to a country day.

7

Saints and Sinners

My recollection of the lady who brightened my leisure by lending me books brings to mind the years between ten and fourteen when I was a member of an important corps of schoolboys called altar boys or 'servers', whose duties were in the big granite church two miles from town.

It was not any particular claim to piety that ensured we were selected for the work. The Master, in conference with the curate, made the selection based on a boy's ability to learn the Latin responses used in the various services, but not necessarily to understand them. A second recommendation for selection was that a candidate's mother would rout him out of bed during 'his week' in time to run to the church and have everything ready for the priest when he stepped over from the parochial house.

When the morning service was over we had to hurry back to town, pick up our satchels and dash back up the long hill to school. As far as the young acolytes were concerned there was no compelling religious vocation. A boy was selected, his mother approved, told him what was required of him and that was that. Like most of my childhood friends I did what I was told. Certainly all altar boys were not on the point of sprouting wings. Several of our band were considered by irate members of the congregation to be young rascals.

We had our favourites among the clergy. The parish priest

who was in charge during my first years among the elite was kind enough to me, and on Sundays gave me a lift to church in a car called a 'Chambers'. I learned that it had been manufactured in Belfast and had some special features that the old pastor required. It soon became evident that the big florid man did not get on well with many members of his flock, though my only painful memory of him is of a morning when, as he was reading the Epistle, I absent-mindedly moved my hand on the carpet and he stepped on it. A good pinch of flesh was caught under the sole of his elastic-sided boot but I dared not utter a sound. Fortunately St Paul's admonitions to the Corinthians on that day were brief.

We liked special occasions in the ecclesiastical year, especially missions, when noted preachers resided in the parish in the parochial houses. Most of the missioners of my childhood were thunderous with disapproval of the shocking state into which the world in general, and our parish in particular, had fallen.

We had to be there to serve during the morning and night services but were not at all worried, for it was adult failings that were being flayed. The pictures of perdition that were painted did not, we were sure, apply to us. Far clearer in my memory than the severest castigation ever meted out to the serried ranks of men and women, segregated in the seats below the pulpit, is the occasion when the big bell went mad and people came to their doors in wonder.

We had reported early for duty at evening devotions. I was a very junior member of the servers' group at the time. The old pastor, aware that the time for the first bell was past, sent me out for the sacristan. I could not find him. The Parish Priest then asked the senior boy if he knew how to ring the bell. The boy, innocent-faced, but known to us as a stern leader and full of tricks, assured him that he did. He was dispatched at once with a young server to the choir loft, fifteen feet above the floor at the back of the church.

The thick bell-rope came down through holes in the floors between the belfry and the choir. It was looped and knotted round the bar of a fifty-six pound weight. When the sexton rang he eased the weight up towards the high ceiling and pulled gently until it came down again, almost reaching the floor. Up it went again a little quicker and higher and down again until the big bell above was dinging and donging rhythmically.

That all was going well with the young ringers was evident, for the first six booms were measured and firm. Then something went wrong and we all stopped to listen. The tolls came loud, then faint, erratically and wildly. All was not well up in the loft. The big man hurried to the vestry door and glared up at the choir. Though far from agile he hastened down the aisle to the loft door and the spiral staircase. From where we stood we could see why. The little white-cassocked boy was clinging to the bell rope, his feet on the weight, his garments flying. Every time he descended the 'fifty-six' thumped the floor and sped up again almost to the roof. The older boy, it appeared, had acceded to his young assistant's request and let him have a go. The older lad had placed the youngster with his feet on the top of the weight and eased him up in orthodox fashion. Carried away by success, it seems that the pulls and pushes became too strong and the little fellow, frightened, clung tightly, rising high and thumping low, until the bell took over.

As the priest mounted the stairs the leader sensed danger and abandoned his assistant, making for the stairs. It is likely that he received a few cuffs as he and the pastor squeezed past one another. At last blessed silence fell on the church and district, and the winded pastor arrived back at base to seek the culprit. He had no success, for the youthful Quasimodo had taken off for other parts. As far as I remember he never again reported for duty.

There were certain worldly benefits to being an altar boy. Occasionally we were told to report during school hours for marriages, christenings and funerals. The last two were run-of-the-mill and got us off school for an hour but assisting at a marriage could augment our pocket money to the extent of a couple of shillings.

In our pre-teen years we did not take much notice of religion as such. It was important, but so much part of daily routine that we did not fuss about it. It was perfectly normal for us to attend our Sunday services and those held to mark special religious feasts during the year. We went on weekdays when required to do so, and were guided by our parents and teachers, with an occasional encouragement from the priest who visited our school.

In our after-school hours at the river or harbour we mixed and played with boys who attended Kilmory and the Meeting schools. Delicate points of theology never arose and we knew nothing of the thorny differences of approach to the Christian faith. They had their notions and we had ours, when we had any notions at all. We were too busy playing to be bothered about such things. We were well aware that there were Protestants and Catholics, that we went to different churches, and that in some way we differed, but it ended there. If the big numbers who attended our church on Sundays spoke well for our particular religion the same could be said for the Presbyterian and Christ Church people, for then, as today, all the churches in our town were well attended.

Because our church was well out of the town and few people had any mechanical means of travel, except the odd bicycle, nearly everybody walked. It was the same with the Protestant churchgoers. Many of their congregations were drawn from the crescent of land round the town and they walked to their places of worship. There were farmers who came in small pony traps or in larger 'fore-and-afters', who were the better-off members of the community. The horse traps that could be seen near the churches were usually fitted with iron hooped wheels, and it was a great advance when solid rubber tyres were fitted over the iron.

When attending our church we carried the traditional aids to fervent prayer, rosary beads and prayer books. Our Protestant friends always carried Bibles. I never saw the inside of one of their bibles, and it seemed to me that reading the bible was a Protestant occupation. I soon realised during our teacher-guided religion lessons in school that part of what we always referred to as 'Catechism' had a fair bit of bible study in it. Each year we had to study and memorise stories from the Old and New Testaments. We liked that part of our course, for all boys like stories. Not so popular was the work on the fat little green catechism where the 'Dos and Don'ts' were set out clearly, but where the follow-up questions were studded with jawbreakers and laced with points of theology obscure enough to drive a boy crazy.

I afterwards learned that the stories in our Protestant friends' Bibles were the same as those we memorised from what we called our Bible Histories. I cannot recall that during my hours, weeks and years of playing and mixing with boys of other faiths I was bothered because they were, in some way, different from me. Whatever the differences that sent us in opposite directions on Sundays and during school hours during the week they seldom manifested themselves when we played or adventured together. It was inevitable, because we seldom saw them between nine in the morning and three-thirty in the evening, that our friendships 'on our side of the house' should be closer and that they should be affected in the same way.

Our district was so cut off from the main centres of secondary education that many boys and girls of all faiths who might have profited from further schooling had little chance to do so. The expense and slowness of travel outside the district ruled out enrolment in the nearest grammar schools and boarding schools in Belfast or Armagh for all but the few.

Fortunately for me and for some of the boys of my age, both Protestant and Catholic, we were cushioned against educational deprivation and the opposite-camps incubus. As our 'teens' opened before us the pastors of the three main churches in our town saw eye-to-eye in the proposition that our isolated district should have a senior school at which all who were willing and able should come together to be taught to matriculation standard. The cost was to be nominal, for the educational authority agreed to take the school under its wing. Not only did the pastors agree on the idea, but they sat down together and planned how they could govern the new school in the interests of all who enrolled.

The school operated successfully for nearly ten years under the inspired and devoted guidance of a pair of graduates and a visiting music teacher, and opened up third level education to boys and girls who would not otherwise have benefited. Perhaps just as important, we of all creeds who attended the school are to this day comfortable in one another's company, able to disagree calmly and work together in friendship.

The rapid development of motorised road transport and the opening of a girls' grammar school near the town led to the run-down and closure of a novel and welcome senior school. We were not aware that grave decisions about our education caused so much concern among adults. We took what was offered, worked hard enough to avoid trouble, and got on with the really serious things in our lives – playing the seasonal games that filled much of our spare time in the long days.

Not all of our free time in summer was spent thus. One thing we had to attend to every day was the carrying of water. Buckets full of the pure, sweet water from what was then called 'Happy Valley' were drawn from the street fountains. These were boy-high cast iron columns, and most efficient.

The top of a fountain was shaped like a helmet with a spike and the bulbous part below was fashioned like a lion's head. At the turn of a knob at the side the water flowed from the animal's mouth. Carrying water could be most unpleasant if buckets were filled to the brim, and if an easy carrying rhythm was not attained wet stockings and full boots could result. We were very much taken with a water-carrying harness put together by the shoemaker whose shop overlooked the river. A light wooden yoke was fitted on to the shoulders, and to this were suspended leather straps with hooks onto which the buckets of water could be hung. Carrying was neater and drier than by the traditional method.

The parents of some of my friends had small fields near the

town or took these at an annual rent for the grazing of a cow or two, and a goat. One of the boys with whom I spent a lot of time had to leave his father's cows out to graze each day and take them in again in the evening for milking. If Micky was not available for the work I sometimes did it for him. It was no trouble, for the docile animals made their way down the street when the field gate was opened, took the right turns and stood at the yard gate until admitted. Traffic problems did not crop up for what little horse-and-cart activity there was left ample room for the cattle. Having a yard, they were able to keep some poultry, and these included a dozen ducks and a drake. Micky saw to it that they enjoyed their habitat, the little river that ran through the town, and the waddling company was conducted each day to the water and back after their ablutions and exercise.

He also kept a couple of hutches of pet rabbits, and allowed me to help with their feeding and grooming. So that they too might enjoy natural surroundings we often carried them to his father's field for a carefully supervised outing. On one such occasion we narrowly escaped parental wrath because of an event that happened through no fault of ours.

Our way to and from the field was past the little oratory at the head of the street. Most people in passing stopped to kneel for a few moments in passing and, presumably, said a prayer. These calls were automatic with all passing girls, and most of the boys broke their journey. We deferred our call until the return with our sack of rabbits.

We placed the living, jerking bag inside the door and moved apart, inducing pious thoughts. Everything was prayerfully still. Then we heard brushing and pattering and rattling from various parts of the little church. Micky had forgotten to tie the mouth of the bag and our charges, all white, all chocolate, chocolate and white, blue and white, black and piebald, were lolloping under the kneeling boards, in the aisle, and in the case of one particularly inquisitive animal, in the confessional. By great good luck we were alone in the place and it was possible to act quickly without too much regard for silence. Alarmed by our efforts to seize and bag them the rabbits took evasive action and made things difficult. One that had disappeared behind the curtain gave most bother for he retreated into a far corner. By the time all but one had been gathered we were convulsed with laughter, all the more painful because of our efforts to suppress it.

As Micky hurried to complete his task the door opened softly and the most sedate lady in the town stepped in. Her astonishment and disgust were understandable for I was bent in two, Micky's legs were projecting from beneath the curtain of the confessional, and he was coaxing an unwilling quarry to return to the fold. She upbraided us for being young rascals and cast doubts on our membership not only of our own faith, but of any other under the Christian umbrella. There was no use in trying to explain so Micky, holding the last rabbit by the ears, followed me to the open air. It was a week before we were easy in our minds about the affair, waiting every day to be charged and punished. We kept well clear of her for a long time and fortunately heard no comment on our fall from grace.

It could hardly be said that our conduct in the oratory deserved the local name for outlawry in the young: rascality. It is a matter of opinion whether or not our forays on fruit patches and orchards near the town were only to be expected in the ripe mellow autumn, or were manifestations of inherent evil. Even at this distance I can say that any scrumping in orchards was prompted neither by badness nor love of ripe fruit. In truth, among my group, anyone who would not take up the challenge of raiding an apple-tree was considered a coward. In every one of the raids in which I was involved I was nervous, for I dreaded that my drift from the straight and narrow would result in my being charged at home with disgracing the family.

Two swoops in which I had a part were followed by periods of worry that cancelled out both the thrill of a successful tilt with danger and the dubious taste of the fruit we obtained. What we called the 'back fields' lay along the river and ran right up to a high wall against which a large hayshed stood, in the form of a lean-to. I am sure that planners did not mean to put temptation in the way of adventurous boys, but the fact remains that hanging over the wall at the top of the slanted roof were the branches of three pear trees.

Our leader had watched the fruit ripening for weeks, and called a conference. He directed that we should shin up to the roof of the shed and then walk up to where the pears seemed to be asking to be picked before they fell. He ordered a henchman to go up to the gate leading into the field and to keep an eye out for anyone who might chance to come up the lane and see us at work. All was going well, so well in fact that the lookout, not wanting to be a mere bystander, joined us in filling pockets and stuffing jerseys.

It might have been all right if, having taken all the pears we could carry, we had not looked down into the garden and seen the rows of currant and gooseberry bushes that were laden with choice fruit. Flushed with success our general was pointing out how easy it would be to share in the treasure below, when we heard a voice directly behind us, at field level.

The venerable, whitebearded gentleman, a pillar of our community, was addressing us, not angrily but in the manner of a counsellor. We listened briefly but did not know what he was saying. Then we broke and scampered down the roof, scrambled and fell to the level and, dropping pears in all directions, headed for the thick hedge that fringed the river. As we disappeared through it the Justice of the Peace (for that is what he was) appealed to us to come back, for he wanted to talk to us.

On the day of that ill-fated raid I was wearing a bright blue jersey and I was sure the gentleman, who sometimes chatted with my great grandfather, must have picked it out for special notice. I could not explain at home why I took such an aversion to wear it. During the same month I never walked past the gentleman's shop when I was sent on errands. I ran as fast as I could; but again I was lucky and escaped detection.

The day I was caught briefly on a gooseberry scrump entailed no danger of recognition although I was as frightened as on the occasion of the purloined pears.

The thing started innocently enough and the garden at the end of our adventure tunnel just happened to be there when we arrived, providing an irresistible temptation. The garden, with the rows of berry bushes, ran down to a field in which we sometimes played on our way to a little coastal glen, rather off our usual route. Between field and garden was a very thick hedge, a dry ditch and about nine feet of undergrowth. We had to stand well back from the hedge to see the big house and lawn at the head of the garden. We knew the name of the people who lived there, a moustachioed man and two tall sisters. We heard they were very musical, and well educated, and that the two ladies had travelled the world as governesses in important families.

Our main thought on that sunny day was to burrow as far as we could into the undergrowth and we made fine progress, for the tangle was not jaggy and the sides and top kept their shape well. As we got deeper we wriggled forward on a nice mat of grass and were delighted when, after climbing a grassy fence, we had only a few more feet to go before we pulled aside the last screen of undergrowth and looked up at the garden. I saw the house, the lawn, and then the man on the summer seat in the shade of the hedge. We decided to wait a day and to have a look at the berries when he had other things to do than sit in the sun, and retreated, blocking both entrances to the tunnel.

All was clear when we came back next day. We acted swiftly, grabbed a couple of pocketfuls of fruit, had a look up at the house and turned to re-enter our bolt hole, only to see the owner standing half way between us and safety. It is likely that he had seen us on our last visit and found the tunnel. I have no idea what he intended for us, but neither of us gave that much thought. We ran straight at the man, splitting as we came close to him. He chose me for arrest.

My friend was already half way across the field to the road gate and soon I was not far behind him. Scrumping went sour after that and it was not because the gooseberries were even sourer; though naturally we boasted to our friends of our foray.

8

The Long Days

Passing the time was never a problem for us: there were far too many things to do in the time available. Energy and interest were in excess of daylight hours even in the long days of summer.

We had few formal games requiring equipment. Leather footballs were rare and goalposts non-existent. Marker stones in the little square or schoolyard served as goals and small nail bags from the cobbler's, well stuffed with paper, were easy on boots. Anyway a goal was a goal, whether or not the ball was inflated.

Our games were seasonal and followed one another with remarkable regularity. As soon as the warm side of the stone turned up on St Patrick's Day there was a rush to search out hoops put away last year. Anything that rolled and could be tapped along by a running boy qualified as a hoop. Rusted bands from fish barrels, thin, light hoops from fruit and meal barrels, midget sized bottoms from worn-out galvanised buckets and even heavy iron hoops from wheelbarrows that required solid thumps to keep them going, all served the running 'hoop men'. On rare occasions members of our 'hoopers' were able to join the 'de luxe corps' when they secured old bicycle wheels, minus the spokes. The propulsion of these required skill and a light touch, for the guide pressed a rounded stick into the wheel groove and worked up to speed and deft manoeuvering.

We looked down on boys whose fathers had made the whole

sport too easy for them by providing them with spoked wheels, sometimes even with the tyres still on. These could be pushed along on rigid wires 'cleeked' through the hubs, and required no skill at all. We dashed and steered up and down the streets, cutting into entries and down loanings to test our abilities. We took our hoops with us on messages. A couple of our band claimed to have completed the four mile round trip to the nearest village.

Quite suddenly, as if on a signal, hoop time was over and when we had time off from catching spricks and looking for nests we started our 'top' season. This occasionally entailed some expense when split tops had to be replaced but usually they lasted for a long time, and some were handed down from generation to generation. I had a very special one that I used only on big occasions, that had belonged to my father.

Usually we spun our tops for the love of hearing them snore in a small circle. A long practised delivery swing could earn a fellow a good name as a top expert, although to achieve perfection it was necessary to wind the grooves of the top with 'nussel cord'. We did not know the origin of the word 'nussel'; in all likelihood it had been coined, and assuredly it was the perfect description for the tightly stranded white linen string. Competition inevitably entered in and skill was judged according to winnings. An oval was marked on the hard clay and stakes of buttons were placed in it. Spins were executed and, if we could make our tops travel and spin buttons out of the ring, they were ours.

As the weather got warmer and it was too hot for running as much as usual the square became the arena for daylong games of marbles. Again we had to buy equipment, but most of us had string bags of marbles left over from the previous season. These included glassies, spheres of multicoloured glass. To us they were useful stakes in our games, but hardly ever used in the real work of running holes and pegging. Somehow they looked too artificial, too dandified for the fray.

The two main types of competition marbles were 'crockeries' and 'flinties' (or 'stonies'). Crockeries were rather fat lifeless things but reliable, ideal for the patient work of getting the holes. The stonies and flinties were lean, quick fighters, about seven-eighths the weight of the trundling crockeries. Our main game of marbles was called 'mugs', and was played by partners who matched themselves against other pairs. It required a level of at least four yards by six yards. Favourite 'mugs' pitches had their edges marked out permanently with grooved border lines. One narrow end of the rectangle was the starting line and was known as the 'butts'. Three small holes were evenly spaced up the middle of the pitch, a couple of yards apart and a yard from the butts. We tossed a halfpenny or a button to decide the order of shooting. One partner in each pair was responsible for getting into the holes (called 'running the holes'), while the other partner, called the 'pegger', and chosen because of the strength and accuracy of his knuckling, shot into strategic positions from which he could scatter other runners and peggers, and safely convoy his runner up the line of holes, down again, and up again for victory.

Much skirmishing ensued with a good deal of argument as the crockeries, like slow lumbering freighters, ploughed on doggedly, taking their knocks, while fleet, tough peggers flashed in at speed, all guns blazing. Intent on our mugs, with the sun on our backs, even a motor car or a motor bicycle could have mounted the brae, or a horse run away, and we would hardly have looked up for fear of breaking the concentration.

The professional element reared its head, even in our marble games, for we had a special one called 'ring of buttons' in which you could not start unless you could show your stakes. We placed our buttons in an oval ring and we tossed for turns. Any button that a boy knocked out of the ring with an accurate speedy marble went into his pocket and he got a second go. If he liked he could satisfy his blood lust by pegging an opponent in lieu of trying for a button. There was no button prize for such a shot, just the joy of sending another man out of the arena. Since there is luck in all these games of chance, and winners and losers, it was inevitable that some players should run out of legal tender and so be excluded from the excitement, for borrowing of buttons from fellow players was frowned upon.

Buttons of various types had their own values. Those with no holes, that were sewed on through central loops, were not buttons at all and gave no right of entry into a game. 'Shirties', the little two holed tiddlers, just qualified for recognition; 'steelies', cut from dungarees, were of medium value; big four-hole 'bonies' from overcoats were first class, but a shade more valuable were 'pearlies', lovely tortoiseshell beauties from ladies' clothing. For that reason the marble season was, for some unfortunates, a time of bad temper for mothers and warm ears and worse for their male offspring. Some boys, desperate for stakes, were driven to attacks with scissors on family coats, skirts and jerseys. Even the winners among us got no joy out of the misfortunes of a 'ring of buttons' addict who had done so badly for so long that he was driven to desperation, running amok with the scissors in the wardrobes. If his bad run continued and he was once again flat broke, and a qualifier for help from 'Buttons Anonymous', it was no comfort for him if his sister brought the message from home that he was 'a wanting'. I recall a particularly rueful case of a lad who had not even a shirty to his name and was sent for. Like mourners at a funeral we followed as he trudged home to his door at dusk. An arm reached out and a voice pregnant with bad temper said:

'Come in here, you ruffian. You have not left a button on your da's good trousers.'

Each year we had a short catapult season. For boys who had strict parents it was often very short indeed, the weapon ending in the fire. We cut our own forks from the hedges and laid hands on rubber from old bicycle tubes with bits of leather for the missile launchers. If boys were in funds they could afford to buy lengths of a very special kind of tubing called 'teat rubber', bought at the druggist's.

In spite of much boasting about kills we did little damage to bird life. Unfortunately our lack of success with live targets resulted in damage to tin roofs, galvanised buckets and sometimes the insulation cups on telegraph poles.

When the river was not running too fast we had a sailing season. Our boats were made out of blocks of wood whittled to shape and fitted with masts and any sails we could get our mothers to cut and sew. Boys whose parents were willing and able to help had excellent craft. We of the boat-sailing community had the benefit of the brains of two boys who lived just across the river and who devised a method of installing engines in toy boats. As a result their house in the fields was the mecca of all who cared enough about the sport to lay hands on the essential equipment.

A sweet that was a great favourite at the time was the butternut, which came in a large oval tin. When empty, it could be opened down the side and the bottom removed, leaving a rectangular piece of tin just right for making the hull of a toy boat. It was then simple enough to cut a piece of thin wood to fit the shaped tin and form the deck of the vessel. The boys we envied used their inventive skill to place below decks, in the stern of the craft, the works of an alarm clock of a type in use in many houses. While the craze lasted no alarm clock in the town was safe. A slender steel shaft was soldered to the mainspring mechanism of the engine and a tin propeller fitted. When the clockwork was wound up and the boat placed in the water it took off for the other side in the manner that delighted the proud owner.

Like most of the people in the town we were starved for mechanical things. Only a few motor cars or motor cycles were seen on our streets. When one stopped we rushed to look at its wonderful construction, and to try to puzzle out the mysteries of the internal combustion engine. We had never seen an aeroplane and even push bicycles were for the few. For that reason we risked the wrath of rural shoppers by picking up bicycles left along the streets and attempting to cycle, leg under the bar, before being overtaken and cuffed.

Most of the shopkeepers had what was called trucks for use in moving bags of meal from their stores to shops. They were strong, low-slung little carriers, moving noisily on the rough streets and pavements. The traders were obliging in lending the trucks to neighbours for the transport of bags of coal or potatoes from stores to homes. Usually all that was required was for the lad to go in and say: 'Please, my mother wants the loan of the truck to go for coal.' If the applicant had a good record for prompt return of the vehicles, permission was given at once, though even with the best of boys their early return was not always guaranteed. A lot depended on the company he had on his errand. There was a temptation to dally and to fit in a quick bit of tobogganing on the river brae or to go for runs round by the cart track with a load of boys rather than a load of coal.

Since the local herring cadgers found the carrying of large wicker baskets of herring on their rounds hard work, some of them put together light hand-carts called 'bogies', made out of soap or butter boxes. Light wooden shafts were fitted at an angle on the top front corners, an axle block stapled on to the bottom, and pram or bicycle wheels fitted to make a vehicle which, even today, with so many prefabricated mechanical toys, would give pleasure to energetic boys. If we could persuade parents to help out with a bogie we were sure of plenty of fun and plenty of company.

In all the street games I recall, which tired us, filled us with joy, and provided the competition we needed for fulfilment, I cannot remember even during the war years that guns had any part, perhaps because they were scarce, expensive and needed a minimum of imagination.

There was little mingling of boys and girls as we played. They skipped incessantly in twos and threes and rhymed as they skipped. They played a skilful game of tossing and catching coloured beach stones, called 'jacks', but the juggling powers required were not for us. Occasionally there came to the fore a girl who could knuckle a marble as well as any of us or even 'cleek', or tap, a speeding hoop with skill, but generally boys and girls played apart. On windy autumn days a seasonal urge came upon us to put together lath and paper kites. There was a sudden run on light packing cases and any thick brown paper the grocer could spare; and string was in demand. We had no need to go out to the fields to send our kites aloft, for we could safely run up the street and allow the air currents between the houses to send our kites cavorting, mounting and sliding. We knew nothing of astronauts or satellites, but were certain that if we could get enough string and the wind was just right, our kite tails could flick the face of the moon.

The long summers are especially clear to me. It seemed that, as there were not many people in our town who had not always been there, everybody knew everybody else, and unannounced visits to neighbours' houses and workshops were taken for granted. Workshops where there was no machinery to drown conversation were friendly places, and there was always a seat, even for a boy who came to look at the craftsmen and to listen to the chaff and banter, the gossip of the workmen.

The cobblers' workshops were cheerful and cosy. Men could work and talk at the same time, shaping soles, flipping knives on sandpapered boards, rolling strands of cotton into tight cords, waxing them to keep them tight, and affixing stiff hog bristles to ensure a clean entry into the leather as they sewed. The speed and rhythm they achieved as they transferred 'sparables' (brass nails) from mouth to sole and hammered them home with two clean strokes always kept my eye glued to them.

Cobblers were fond of news and were particularly interested

in snippets passed on by country men who came in with jobs and waited until they were completed. Not every home took a newspaper but the cobblers were kept abreast of events in the outside world by the shop-owner who, if he had free time, leaned against the wall and read to his staff. Even young folk who were considered to be good scholars were asked to read from local weekly papers. The resulting argument, debates and discussions could last for hours.

In the saddler's shop, with its smell of leather and background of birdsong (for the saddler was a breeder of canaries), I heard a story that made me more determined than ever to keep far away from the ancient cemetery after daylight. The man telling the yarn chuckled and his listeners laughed quietly but I, silent in the corner listened intently. They talked of the journeyman saddler who, on his ramblings over the counties sometimes stopped for a month or two in the town to follow his trade before the wanderlust drew him away. He was fond of drinking, and the more he imbibed the braver he became, breathing defiance of anything on two feet, or even four.

One Hallowe'en he was fit to face anything, and took up the challenge of his cronies at the nearby public house to climb the wall and walk alone in the graveyard, bringing back a memento of his visit as proof of his fearlessness. The wind roared round 'the church of the narrows', tossing the branches and lashing the place with showers of cold rain. The little man was helped up the ten foot wall, hooked his elbows on the granite curb and pulled himself up, falling in a heap in the long wet grass. He groped and stumbled forward tripping on slabs and cannoning into headstones, but doggedly made his way to the ruined walls of the church and, though afraid, to the far boundary of the place. On his way back his troubles began. It was told as follows:

'When I was groping about for something to bring back I heard these voices, one from the right and then another from the left, one in front of me and, the worst of all, behind me. If I touched anything somebody would say in a desperate voice: "Don't touch that. That belongs to my aunt." Another would say: "Don't dare put your hand on that. It belongs to my grandfather." Then there would be another shouting: "Take your hand out of that. That's my granny's."'

His listeners knew he was not exaggerating for while he was climbing into the cemetery they had posted men at different points to provide the ghostly voices. Nevertheless they extended their sympathy and asked if he had answered back. He said he had, before he made his way to safety, and had said to whoever they were: 'Bad luck to yez, yez can't all be related.'

A favourite place of call was the home of the jolliest, kindest woman of my youth. Minnie lived with her family in a warm little house right up against the cemetery. Our interest in the ruined walls and quiet place had nothing to do with its history. Naturally, because it was out of bounds and shut off by a high wall and a spiked gate, it offered a challenge. Our main interest in visiting it was that in the middle of the tangle of high grass there was an ancient, granite tombstone with a hole hollowed out of it, known as 'the Wart Pan'.

It seems to me that today's children are singularly free of warts but I remember that we always had a few boys at school who could boast of knuckle crustations. If any boy in our company had warts he was very foolish if he did not avail of the sure curative powers of 'The Wart Pan'. We veterans of past pilgrimages were ready and willing to accompany a wart-afflicted boy at any time, except after dark on a winter's night. We played on Minnie's sympathy and coaxed her to assist in illegal entry into the churchyard. She spread a newspaper on her oil-clothed kitchen table below a tiny window that was just on a level with the cemetery. One by one we wriggled through. The ritual was simple but very earnest. The patient bathed his warts thoroughly in the rusty water in the pan and dropped in his pins to join the pile that lay in the bottom of the cup. We closed our eyes and willed, with all the power we had, that the warts disappear. They never did, on the first instant, but our faith was always rewarded, for they would shrivel and eventually vanish.

9

Travelling People

The outstanding architectural feature of our town was the big square block of red brick buildings by the side of the long school hill. It stood in its own grounds, and had a 'shut-in' appearance. We could not fail to notice it for we passed it each day on our way to school or when we went to the chapel. Its quarter-mile frontage was bounded by a high granite wall pierced by two gates in the front, one black and one red.

At the upper corner on the street was a neat little building that looked like a cottage but which was known as the 'Dispensary', a place nobody visited unless he had to. In fact it was a kind of old-fashioned clinic which a doctor attended a couple of times a week. I heard, but did not understand that people went there to get a 'line'. This meant that anyone who could not afford to call a doctor to his home could get a note from the dispensary doctor entitling him to free medical attention.

As we were always in a hurry going to school, and in a greater hurry on the way home, we had little thought of what went on inside the walls of the big institution. In time we learned that it existed because of sickness and poverty, and that it was needed in the lamentable conditions that existed in our land.

While we sometimes took our courage in our hands and climbed to the top of the wall for look between the high Scots pines that bordered the place, the walls itself and the gloomy look of the trees were effective deterrents for inquisitive boys. We knew that in one wing was the hospital for ordinary people but that away at the back was a two-storeyed place set out by itself for something dreadful called fever that affected certain people who were sent there. Some boys who thought they knew all about the workings of the place referred to the isolated building as 'the fevery hospital'.

With outbreaks of diphtheria and scarlet fever all too common at the time, the fever unit was seldom empty. The part that intrigued us most was what was slurringly pronounced 'the workis' or 'the pooris', a place for paupers, for homeless ones.

The big rubicund man whom we saw in front of the main door where the big laburnum tree drooped over a circular patch of grass was 'The Master'. He and his wife were in charge of the place and saw to its efficient running. The energetic little wife whom we saw regularly at the chapel dealt with a corps of orderlies and trusted inmates, and saw that the men, women and children who were in permanent sanctuary were fed, housed and looked after. Some of them were unable to work and often there was nothing for them to do except keep the grounds tidy, clean and help with household work.

Ours was one of a chain of such institutions throughout the country. On certain occasions during the year, a migratory influx of rambling people filled the dormitories to capacity. Tramps were plentiful in the country at that time and the district was seldom without its wanderers. Farmhouses and cottages had their callers in quest of alms and they were seldom turned away. They did not always get cash; more often being offered bread or cast-off clothing.

There is no doubt that though most of the beggars were grateful for gifts in kind there was a hard core that preferred money to help them forget their miseries in drink. On such occasions as the monthly fair and cattle market or commemoration holidays the workhouse was full for days. Tramps and beggars, anxious to cash in on the extra money that was sure to be in circulation, begged in the town and its environs before the big day, passed the night in the workhouse, and spent the following day mixing with farmers and country workers on the streets asking for money and accepting any drink that might be offered. Without exception they were a pitiful company, almost bootless and with clothes in tatters. Sometimes there would be family groups with infants wrapped in mothers' shawls and even more frequently loners, without roots, without hope, literally living from hand to mouth and totally dependent on the charity of others.

I never heard that destitute folk were blamed for stealing and, except in cases when they had had too much to drink, they were never violent. They were hapless, hopeless creatures with no fight left in them. They expected little and got little, accepted a gift or a refusal with a shrug. Their very existence was a disgrace to our land, a reproach to every one of us. Even the young among us sensed this. That is why, in our town, as in others, the young felt uncomfortable in their presence but not afraid of them. Neither we nor our elders would have dreamed of saying when they knocked and waited: 'Go away. I have nothing for you.'

So regularly did the same tramps return to our town that it seems they found their visits well worthwhile. Key figures among the vagrants were known to the people and, though nobody knew their names, they were nevertheless recognised at once.

There was one exception, whose name was known to everyone, and he made sure that people did not forget him or confuse him with the 'common-or-garden' tramps. The main occupation of his life seemed to be to disguise the fact that he ever did or ever could ask for alms, and he never missed a Fair Day. His name was a curious one and it was hard to see why he was so called because he was never without a hat. Tommy Barewig (Barewig, for short) was a dandy, though every item of his wardrobe was a hand-me-down and often so threadbare as to be ready to fall to pieces.

Somehow he turned himself out so well, making the best of what he had, that he gave the impression he had the help of a valet while dressing. From the shine on his face and his trimmed black moustache it looked as if he washed carefully. He usually had a stiff collar and was never without a tie of sorts. He always wore an overcoat, winter and summer, which came down to within four inches of his boot tops, and his trousers, though the worse for wear, were never 'concertinaed'. It was said that he used stove polish for his battered boots for ordinary boot blacking could never have given the metallic shine he achieved. And though his walking stick was obviously out of the hedge, he carried it with an air and it looked elegant in his hand. There was a rumour that he had been a policeman, not just one who walked a beat, but in the 'plain clothes' department. So another name for the unique character was 'the detective'. I think he encouraged the belief in his past eminence.

It was a measure of his distinction in the wandering band that it was not necessary to call him Tommy. Refer to him by his surname and everybody knew who was meant: there was only one Barewig. It was a sign that, among the homeless ones, he was regarded as being a step above the rest on the social ladder. He was a loner, seldom fraternising with the common herd. When they were about he managed to create the impression that he was in town on business that had nothing to do with tramps. Had there been a guild of the homeless it is certain that Barewig would have been elected father of the chapel without opposition.

As well as the tramps who came to fairs there was a more select band of entertainers who worked for any money they could get from the people on the streets. There were so few public entertainers that performers did well, for the country men loved a song, dance or novelty act.

It must be admitted that some of the acts they presented were lamentably poor but that did not matter to the folk who stopped and gathered round. Sometimes they combined a bit of business with the acts and used the latter to attract a crowd so that they could sell the sheets of ballads and small knick-knacks such as studs, button-hooks and bootlaces. At certain fairs the well known almanac, *Old Moore's*, was sold widely by the entertainers. It was highly prized in country homes for it listed the dates of all the fairs in Ireland, gave the times of tides, phases of the moon and columns of riddles and jokes as well as selections from the prophecies of St Columcille. Nearly every farmhouse and fisherman's dwelling had an *Old Moore's*.

The fair performers spaced themselves out over the town so that none would intrude on the other's pitch. For years two very tall skinny men came to every fair to sing. They looked like brothers and wore wide hats and long-skirted coats. For some reason they had the names 'Flirty' and 'Skirty'. I wondered why, when they sang, they put their hands to the sides of their mouths. It could not have been to make them audible for in all the years I heard them singing I could not make out more than a little of what they were saying.

An old bearded man with a fiddle and a young girl with a harp were great favourites because they were good performers, and their items made everybody stop to listen and give generously. We also had a good performer on the mouth organ, and a man with a melodeon who set feet tapping with jigs and hornpipes; men who blew fire from their mouths. One with tattoos on his arms and chest who said he was a sailor drew the men round him when he lay on the ground allowing a flat stone to be broken on his chest with a sledge hammer.

The favourite with all the boys was the man who never sang anything but *The Gallant Forty-Twa*, which dealt with the fighting qualities of a Highland regiment. He changed his location to different parts of the town but we followed him and, while his singing was not of a high standard, we thought his marching and drilling good enough for a Guards' squad. The round pole on his shoulder was his rifle, and he paced with military precision over a distance of a dozen yards, turned with stamping feet and paced back again, giving himself orders that he obeyed like a Palace sentry. He sang while he worked us up to fever pitch, keeping time to the song with his movements. It all worked to a climax we liked when, on the last word of the song, he dropped to one knee, levelled his rifle and let off a simulated volley. Then he rose, stood straight as a ramrod, and saluted. He did not hurry round with the cap, but always got plenty of coppers. From what I remember of the song, the chorus went something like:

You may talk about your Irish Guards
And British Grenadiers,
Your own brave Inniskillings
And your Dublin Fusiliers,
Or any other regiment that's gang far awa'
But give to me the soldiers of the gallant Forty-Twa.

Unless the fair-day fell during school holidays, we had to wait impatiently until the Master gave us permission to leave half an hour earlier than usual. Schoolmates whose fathers were farmers were excused if they took the day off, to help marshall the stock from the farm to town. Farmers joined forces to herd cattle and sheep along the country roads and to prevent them bolting up loanings and over hedges. It was in this work that the sprightly schoolboys were so useful. They ran ahead of the flocks, darted through gaps and, as we said, 'capped' the straying animals.

All sales took place on the streets. Corners and entries were crowded with animals and the sidewalks were blocked. Pink piglets in the carts of the Newry and Dundalk breeders, who had brought them in to restock our sties, were on display so that the farmers could judge the quality of the animals. It was also common to see a ram and a couple of ewes roped by the horns and pulled in close to public house doors so that bargains could be sealed in the traditional fashion, with treats. As the bars were crowded all day it seemed that haggling was thirsty work and that throats needed frequent lubrication.

The crowds in public houses did not mean that our people were intemperate, merely that their visits to town were infrequent. Drinking, mostly of stout and whiskey, was not a day-in, day-out practice. We were scared of drunk men but they were not a common sight either on fair days or at any other time.

From time to time there would be a commotion on the street with much shouting and closing in of spectators. We always kept well away from such centres of trouble but often enough, from the high footpaths on our main street, we could see men wrestling, shouting and striking. The police, whom I remember as tall strong men, not carrying guns but with batons in leather scabbards by their sides, were frequently called in to separate fighters. If they resisted and continued to fight they were seized by the arms and dragged to the police barracks. So strong were some of the intoxicated men that the police had to use three men to move them up the street. Even then it was necessary to 'put the screws' on them, twisting their arms half-way up their backs. We did not know what happened when the barracks was reached, but it was reported that the fighters were thrown into the 'Black Hole' for the night. Our idea of this fearsome place was that it had a trap door and was quite black.

Stories of hard men who, in being frog-marched to the barracks proved themselves 'hard to take' and who, though outnumbered, gave as much as they got to the constabulary, entered the folklore of the district.

The 'Wee Crusher' distinguished himself in a memorable tussle instigated, it was said, by a sergeant of indomitable will and no tolerance at all of insubordination. The Crusher had arrived from County Mayo to work at the early excavations at Silent Valley. From the outset he had double trouble for, though strong as a Clydesdale, he was only five feet four, while his wife was at least a foot taller; and he had got on the wrong side of the sergeant. He walked four and a half miles each day to the mountain workings, performed the hard labour there diligently and well, and thought he deserved a few pints at the close of the day. If, when he felt like it, he burst into loud song and threw in the occasional echoing whoop it was not thought by anyone, except the sergeant, that he was doing much harm.

It happened that, on a fair-evening, the sergeant heard the happy Crusher singing and whooping, and ordered him to vacate the pub and proceed home at once. The Crusher did not see why he should, the policeman collared him and ejected him. Then a fierce struggle ensued on the pavement, with first the six foot tall sergeant on top and then the little bantam of a labourer. They rolled and wrestled until a constable was alerted, and he called out one of his fellows. The Crusher was dragged to his feet, but the struggle was by no means over, for the little man could be moved only a yard at a time. Indeed, the policemen had to sit on him from time to time to regain their strength. The sympathy of the onlookers was with the Crusher for they thought he did not deserve what he was getting, and they admired his strength and spirit. Eventually the door of the barracks closed behind him and a last whoop rang in the street.

It was said that he incurred the full penalty of the law and was given a three month sentence. His stay in the district was short and he never returned to what was then called Happy Valley. Yet many remembered him much longer than the sergeant.

It was amusing to go round the fair listening to the buyers and the farmers haggling over cattle. There would be offers, walking away, pulling back by friends, further offers and more walking away. Finally, there would be much hand-slapping to seal the bargain and requests for 'luck pennies', small hand-backs of money from the agreed price.

There was a man in our town who did not keep cattle, but who sometimes had a cow for sale in the fair. Apparently, if he heard that an old cow was on her last legs he would start out early in the morning, walk to the farm and offer to take the animal off the farmer's hands. Even the farmers were surprised at times at being offered anything for such animals. If the townsman could get his purchase as far as the town, allowing her to stop frequently to rest and graze briefly by the roadside, there was always the chance that he could find a buyer and be paid for his walk and his patience.

We saw him one day with his cow at the Meeting House wall. She looked ready to drop and her eyes were closed. Maybe it was too sunny for her. We heard a buyer from outside the town addressing the man.

'Is she for sale?'

'What do you think I'm standing here for – my health?'

'How much do you want for her?'

'It is you that wants to buy. What will you offer?'

'I'll give you thirty bob for her.'

There was a laugh from some men who had stopped to listen to the sport. This put the seller in a bad temper and he said quietly, but as if he meant it:

'Go away and boil your head, Barney.'

'All right, don't lose your temper. Here, give me your hand. I'll give you the two pounds for her.'

'Look, Barney. You're wasting your time. I wouldn't waken her for it.'

We did not wait to see the outcome, but a bargain must have been struck, for we saw our man going home shortly afterwards, without his cow.

We looked forward to the free entertainment and excitement of the fair-days because the town had few organised entertainments and the chances of keeping up with developments in the musical and dramatic worlds were few. There may have been some privileged people who travelled outside the district to attend concerts or performances of plays. If they did it did not make much impression on the group of children of which I was a member.

Somebody did mention that a boy we knew, the son of a hardware merchant, had gone on holidays to Switzerland. As a result a couple of us looked up the place the next time we were pointing out places on the map. We found its location but there was little detail to be seen for the country had been pointed out of existence by a generation of past pupils. As we knew the boy's father was rich we lost interest, for thc chanccs of our ever having a holiday in Switzerland were not bright.

When we did have a chance of entertainment we relished it to the full and because we had to pay, made sure we squeezed the last drop of pleasure out of it. The arrival of circuses from towns outside the mountain range were high spots of our summer pleasure. The circus season lasted from early June to the middle of August but our weeks of anticipation were nearly as good as the actual shows; and the follow-up to the big tent shows gave us an extra month of acting out what we had seen.

Only one of the circuses that brightened those years had an Irish sound about it and that was 'Duffy's' but, when we got close to the circus people, they all talked with English accents and even more foreign ones. I remember the circus names much better than the names of many notables of the time probably because the days under the high canvas domes were so full of colour and excitement. We had 'Hannaford's', 'Poole and Bosco's' and 'Lloyd's'. The names seemed to us to be just right for such wonderful shows.

As soon as the posters announcing their forthcoming arrival were pasted up on the walls we planned that on the day of the circus we would ask to be wakened early so that we could go along the road to meet the big covered wagons, the barred trailers with the animals in them, and the strings of horses and ponies that were not even tethered, but wandered all over the road as the circus made its way to the selected field.

We waited until the last moment before dashing off to school to watch the positioning of wagons and caravans, and making a start on raising the tent. If we were allowed to give a hand hauling on a rope or throwing an armful of straw to the horses we felt part of the wonderful company. Any boy who, because he had been noticed helping with the work, was given a free pass to the daytime performance, was in his high heaven.

The joy of circus day was double if it happened to come on a Saturday or during the school holidays, for it meant that we could spend every moment in the field dodging round the caravans and carriages and, in the yet unseated tent, revelling in the magical atmosphere created by sunlight filtering through green canvas on to what had been a patch of grass in an empty field a short time before. The strange children in the vans, the odd accents, the big dark-eyed woman with enormous gold earrings, the little stoves with outsize teapots and sizzling pans, and the curtained alcove bunks were things we did not see every day.

No expense was spared by the circus men to ensure the tent would be full at both performances. They put on a parade of nearly all the circus personnel, intimating even greater delights in the big top itself: red, yellow and green carriages, clowns, jugglers on flat drays, beautiful sequinned ladies, acrobats and wirewalkers pirouetting and waving, a man on stilts made taller by his stovepipe hat, a real Pied Piper of a man in his domino costume, making the people lining the streets laugh as he peeped through high windows, cowboys and Indians riding peaceably together, and enough horses to equip a cavalry regiment. The drumming and blaring from the packed bandwagon were enough to make everybody want to stop work for the day and follow the parade.

The matinée performance was the most we could hope to see. To be taken to the night performance by an uncle or a male neighbour was the ultimate in delight for, though the show might start before dusk, night fell well before it finished, and the acts which enthralled us in daylight hours were magic after dark. For excitement nothing could compare with the swinging lanterns, wavering kerosene flares, the shadows on the roof of the high tent, the wooden seats close to the ring where you could almost touch the big horses as they passed with the two or three children balancing on their backs, the performing dogs, the midget ponies doing tiny jumps, the capering clowns who, you hoped, would not pick you out to do anything, the strong man with enormous muscles raising barbells above his head and challenging anybody to match him, trapeze girls making our hearts stop as they just caught the bars and no more, the knife thrower, the cowboy spinning his lasso, the Indian attack on the lurching stagecoach and, behind it all, the music of the band reverberating in the canvas dome.

The excitement carried over long after the tent was folded and the caravans and carriages trundled away while we slept in the small hours of the morning. We always went back to the field to look at the trampled grass and the horse-trodden ring where so much had happened. There was a feeling of loss as we paced the forsaken field. Yet out of the circus visits we distilled hours of pleasure with our home-made lassos, bows and arrows, feather bonnets and stilts, acting out what we had seen.

Among us was a boy who, given the chance, could have put his flair for showmanship to good use in the outside world. As it was he made do by selecting the best of us to assist him in putting on miniature circuses in the biggest hayshed he could find. He was ringmaster and doorman, and he made many an honest penny and button out of our barked shins, bruised elbows and warm ears.

The town was on the 'tent show' circuit, and nearly every year we had a visit from travelling players who came to perform their plays. The tent was much smaller than that of the circus, with a stage rigged at one end. The seats were ranged in front of it, the more expensive in the front costing one shilling and sixpence, while those at the back, rising in a tier, could be had for ninepence.

The small company of players, eight at most, tackled dramas that required up to a dozen actors in their original casting. The result was that the man acting a doctor, for example, in the first act, had to come on in the second as the father of the fair maiden who had been wronged by the son and heir of the gentleman of the Big House. Nobody minded at all.

I can never remember seeing a funny play in one of the old

tents. They all had lots of tears and the older people, who never missed the performances, wanted it that way. So *East Lynne* and *Maria Martin*, the only two that I recall clearly, often had to be repeated during the company's stay with us. The boys of my group were not that keen on the shows but, because they were in a tent, we never missed them if we could afford the admission price.

Open air shows, set in a field in the middle of the town, stayed longer and were well patronised. They suited us well, for swings on the boats and chairplanes were cheap. Most of our pleasure from these shows came from running round the stalls and attractions, and playing to the music of the big steam organ that grunted and wheezed from dusk until nearly midnight. There were many 'table games' laid out on the field, though we were far too careful with our pennies to throw them away on gambling. The shooting galleries attracted us but even at three shots a penny we could not afford to throw away money for the sake of hearing the little bell behind the white disc ping as a bull's eye was scored.

One evening I got so involved in the excitement and fun of the fairground that I risked a whacking, duly administered, for staying out too late. I was about to go home when I witnessed an extraordinary incident involving the tallest person I had ever seen and a showman.

I knew the tall man was a 'Yank' – a name we applied to men from our district who had returned after spending years working in the United States. He wore a wide-brimmed hat, trousers specially cut with a low waist and a buckled belt that I envied, and a coloured bow-tie.

Knowing he was a Yank I was sure he knew a lot, having travelled in distant places. He was a quiet man and hardly spoke once during the course of his disagreement with the showman. The latter set up a little table in the field, took out a pack of cards and began to shuffle them and perform tricks with them as if they were on elastic. It was not long before he was surrounded by a ring of men.

The showman began to call out for cardplayers while he selected three cards from the pack. He threw these on the table so that they fell apart, face down. Then he turned them up and we saw that one was a queen; he referred to her as 'the lady'. He threw again and asked if any of us knew where she was. I knew and so did my friend who had managed to get in close to the table. The showman looked at me and then at the boy beside me and said he was sure the little boy could find the missing lady. The boy pointed and there she was. He did it again and I pointed to the back of the card, and was right. The third time the youth who pointed her out was wrong, for when the card was turned up it was not the queen. My friend was right on the next throw, however, and the man said: 'Good boy. You have a sharp eye. Now, gentlemen, if the boy can spot her so can you. Who'll bet me a shilling I cannot fool you?'

He flipped the cards again and a man behind me pointed and said:

'That's her.'

'Put up your money then, and if you are right you win a bob.'

The country man put down his shilling and won.

On the next throw there were two bets of a shilling and both lost. I found it most puzzling for I was sure that the men had chosen the right card.

A few more men were betting now and it seemed as if they were getting the better of the showman The Yank had joined in a couple of times and won. Still flipping the cards and crossing his hands the showman continued to talk and smile.

'You are too many for me, but I feel lucky and I'll take any bets that are going on the throw. Come on now, you have my money so why not risk it. It's your brains against my hands.'

He threw the cards and waited. Shillings and a couple of half crowns were placed, all on the one card. It was not the lady.

'Hard luck men, I told you I was lucky. I'll not run away, but give you another chance. Here goes.'

The cards lay on the table and he turned away to talk to a man behind him. As he did so someone near me lifted the edge of a card and showed us the lady, though he bent it a little before the showman turned back to the game.

'No bets?' he asked. 'That suits me. Maybe you looked when my back was turned. Here we go again.'

To everybody's disappointment he lifted the cards and went through his routine again. All our eyes were fixed on the table, and sure enough, there was the lady, with the mark where the bend had been still clear.

'Get your bets down, gentlemen. This is my last throw.'

The money came down quick and fast, all on the marked card.

'I doubt you are out to destroy me,' said the showman, 'but I brought it on myself. Any more bets before I turn the card?'

The Yank, who had been waiting his chance to place a really large bet, took his wallet from his hip pocket and I got a glimpse of a thick wad of notes. He took two of them and put them on top of all the silver. Then the showman pulled the card out and turned it. It was not the lady.

He pocketed the cards and the money and offered all the losers his sympathy. He was about to fold his table to go when the big Yank, who had not spoken throughout the game, brought his toe up from under the table and lifted it off the ground.

The showman said nothing but stooped for the table and made off quickly. So did I for it was long after dark. I was told by friends in school the next day that the showman had set up his table a couple more times in different corners of the field, but that each time the big Yank had appeared out of the darkness and repeated his kicking act. Although the show remained for a couple of weeks after that, the showman with the missing lady took no part in it.

The advent of 'pictures', moving pictures, to our town revolutionised the entertainment scene and a new world of wonder was opened to us. We had pictures before we had electric light. They were first shown early in the War years when an Englishman, his wife and daughter came to live in the town. We heard he had been a showman somewhere and soon the word got out that he had taken over the top floor of a big store, up one of our side loanings.

We were allowed to go to Saturday matinées, climbing steep steps to see the modern miracle. The 'machine', as it was called, was placed at the back of the hall, its beam focussed on a white sheet at the other ed. There was no attempt at hiding its 'innards' for when we looked at the screen we were sometimes behind the level of the machine and sometimes to the side, and we could both see and hear the operator cranking the film through by hand. The light was supplied by an early kind of bottled gas, the film passing the lens within terrifying distance of the naked flame.

It was in the loft of the big potato store that I first met Charlie Chaplin, the comic policeman, Fatty Arbuckle, Douglas Fairbanks, and assorted cowboys. The serials that kept on for weeks were what we really liked. We could hardly endure the wait to see how the heroes would get clear of the fixes they found themselves in each Saturday. They always did, and neither avalanche, snake pit, volcano, cliff top nor gorilla had power to defeat the new wonder men.

A particular favourite among the serials wrought havoc among our loose coins. It was called *The Broken Coin* and was about important information and buried treasure. The information was inscribed on a coin that, for security reasons, had been cut in half. Most of us had broken coins, broken with the family hatchet, and buried all over the place, although the messages we scraped on them are hardly lively to cause a flutter in archaeological dovecotes if turned up in future diggings.

There were no censors in our town though some people were not happy about this moving picture business. They knew that 'the devil had many ways of going about his work'. We were not concerned with ratings however – 'A', 'AA', 'U' and especially 'X' and I have never thrilled to the products of the film industry as I did to the offerings in Bolger's loaning picture palace.

10

The Closing Years

Our favourite autumn game was 'linty'. I never found out how it got its name. It was simplicity itself as far as equipment was concerned; the only necessity was an empty two pound 'Golden Syrup' tin. This was ideal in size and in plentiful supply because the delicious refined syrup it contained was used in many households. It was easily spread and topped to perfection slices of either baker's or mother's bread. So much so that a hungry boy, let loose with fresh, salted butter and a tin of syrup could do away with the greater part of a loaf or bannock with amazing speed.

Empty tins provided hours of activity and fun on autumn nights when the darkness fell earlier, and added extra excitement to our 'linty'. It was the ideal dusk game. A linty muezzin would call the faithful from the wall in front of the school: 'All in for a game of linty! All in for a game of linty!' And we came running to join him.

Lots were drawn to select 'a man to go on the tin'. He set it in the middle of the square, put his foot on it, covered his eyes with his hands, and gave us a brief period to conceal ourselves. There were plenty of places to hide at a reasonable distance from the 'tin man'. We could choose the pile of bricks or the stack of timber outside the big store. There was the wall running in front of the Hollow with steps at either side, and good cover. If we liked we could nip round the back of the school and come out at the river end. When we were ready he sallied here and there, always keeping within running distance of his base.

Linty was a game that demanded honesty if it was to be a success. Thus, when the tin man spotted one of us, called out the name and was right in his call, it was incumbent on the unfortunate victim to take his place as a prisoner near the tin. The excitement grew as the tin man made successful calls and only a few were left in hiding.

If he ventured too far there was always the chance that a well-hidden man who had managed to creep close would beat the guard in the run to the tin and kick it far from its spot, releasing a horde of yelling prisoners. I have scored points and kicked goals over the years, but have yet to savour a thrill equal to that of booting a tin twenty yards down the river brae, and hearing it rattle and roll to the accompaniment of yelps of joy from my fellow linty men.

While we did not like the honour, we duly accepted our places on the tin and played the game until the oil lamps in the shop windows made the darkness even darker and voices called us in for the night. The oil lamp darkness was, strangely, a charm of our times. It gave a sense of cosiness, closeness and safety if we were within the lighted area. We avoided going outside it and our night excursions were more restricted than those undertaken when the long hours of daylight were with us. Running up Bolger's loaning, round by the Mill loaning or over the Cart Track were trips that were never made, even in company, when the darkness drew in early.

It was late in October and almost dark when a neighbouring butcher, having none of his boys about the place, asked me to run an errand for him, delivering a parcel of beef at a house some distance away. He gave me clear directions yet I was uncomfortable about the commission, for the house was off my usual beat. I hurried to get the job over, because I could not see a friend to accompany me, and must have passed the place. He had said that it was large and that I could not miss it for there were heavy growths of ivy on either side of the front door. I turned back as I came to the last house in the street and saw the place I was looking for. Sure enough there was the ivy and the heavy knocker.

As I paused a book I had been reading flashed across my mind. I had seen it on my great-grandfather's shelf for a long time but thought it was too dull and fat to be interesting. The name of the author, Dickens, took my fancy, however, spurred me to open the volume, and I had made my first acquaintance with *Great Expectations*. After flipping through it at random I read about Pip and his encounter with the poor convict from the hulks, about genial Joe Gargery and then about the boy's entry to the deserted courtyard and his first sight of weird, shrunken Miss Havesham. It was really Miss Havesham who was responsible for what happened after I had lifted the knocker of the dark hall door and let it fall with a thud.

There was no light in the place and I was hoping there was nobody in so that I could run back to the butcher. Then I saw a wavering light above me through the fanlight. A door creaked inside and a bolt was drawn back. I stood back as the door opened very slowly, after sticking at the bottom. Directly in front of me and framed against the darkness of the long hall was a tall lady with a candlestick at shoulder level. The breeze caught the flame so that it swayed and flickered, highlighting her brow and cheeks, but making dark shadows of her eyes. She was looking straight at me and I thought she grimaced, though perhaps she was smiling. Her hair was pulled back very tightly behind her ears. She bent forward, not speaking. Neither did I.

I put the parcel of beef forward nervously and she said something. I did not catch her words. Then the memory of Pip, the convict, the faded candlelit room and Miss Havesham were too much for me. Involuntarily I threw the parcel into the darkness and fled down the long street and, at last, into our lighted kitchen. My mother settled me with kind words and assured me that the lady whom she knew well was not in the least strange, that in fact she was the soul of kindness. She impressed on me the danger of letting my imagination run away with me. There was never any complaint to the butcher and I assumed that what I had done had scared the good woman as much as she had scared me.

When we were in groups and the lights were lit we loved to be allowed to stay out an extra hour. We had not yet reached the stage when, at Hallowe'en, there was an outburst of 'pranking' involving such activities as removing gates, carts and wheelbarrows, and leaving them in odd places. A bucket was occasionally up-ended on a chimney pot with uncomfortable consequences and there was a run on cayenne pepper and cotton wool, so that cottagers could be 'stoved out' when the smouldering mixture was placed under the crack at the bottom of the door.

We contented ourselves with wearing home-made false faces, knocking on doors and parading with candles in scooped out turnips, that resembled skulls. We spent most of Hallowe'en night at home dipping for apples in the tub, trying to bite the red-cheeked fruit as it hung from a cord, and clearing plates of apple pies and dumplings that might contain threepenny bits or, by a stroke of luck, a sixpence.

Delayed reaction to one Hallowe'en prank gave me one or two days of worry. On the day after the Feast we were exploring the riverbank near the town bridge when we came upon a gate which obviously belonged to the school and which had been heaved over the high wall on to the grassy bank. One of us thought it a pity that the pranksters had not succeeded in their objective of throwing the gate into the river and suggested we finish the job. We concurred and, seizing a corner each and working up a rhythm, we landed the gate in the pool.

Our genius said that was far too simple for the gate could easily be seen, so it was incumbent on us to camouflage it by throwing small stones on top. The work was going well when we heard a stern voice from the bridge above. It was a man with a black moustache whom our leader dismissed as unimportant because he had nothing to do with the school. Engrossed in our work we looked up again a little later. This time we continued looking, for the river wall was lined and in the middle of the spectators was the tall master from Kilmorey School. Though we had no experience of him we knew from listening to Church of Ireland friends that he was a terror, and not easily fooled. Worse than that, he was a crony of my great-grandfather.

He ordered us to come up at once. It never occurred to us to disobey, so we trooped along the bank and up the sharp little hill to street level. Some of the onlookers on the bridge drew near to hear what was being said but he told them to move away. I was in terror and the boys around me were most uncomfortable. Our leader kept his head and, as we neared the Master he narrowed his eyes, but instructed out of the corner of his mouth: 'Cry, boys.'

Most of us were on the point of tears anyway, and needed little urging. I could see that our leader was setting a fine example, for if he was not in tears he was snuffling and giving a worthy performance. It worked too, even with the experienced master and though his words sent shivers through us, the stern pedagogue was softened, and merely told us, in so many words, to go away and sin no more.

One Hallowe'en two of my friends had a marvellous stroke of luck. They found a banknote. This was, to them, a once-in-a-lifetime happening, for I am sure they had never had so much money before, just for the frittering away. The senior of the boys had a sweet-eating ambition in life. He usually made do with a bag of lozenges or a handful of peppermint chunks but he was hooked on an expensive, refined sweet, a gum that came in a large oval box, and could never get enough of them. Here was his chance to indulge himself and he decided, with the agreement of his friend, that if the money covered the price of a whole tin he would buy it.

He came back out of Hagan's with the tin in his arms and I saw to my amazement that it was nearly full. It was well after my bedtime but he told me to eat away as there was plenty for everybody. The addict did not report for school next day. His friend did and confessed that he never wanted to see one of the gums again. He told me that the absent boy had not been feeling well when he called for him on the way to school. In addition his mother had thought she would have to send for the doctor because his jaws, ('the hinges of them', as he put it) had swollen up and she thought he had lockjaw.

Though such incidents were of more interest to us than the things that excited older folk we shared the sorrow of a tragedy that occurred just off our coast on a November night during the War. The story of the collision of the steamers *Retriever* and *Connemara* became part of the folklore of a people whose lives are touched by the sea in all its moods.

Often when our activities took us to the sea bank near the harbour we saw the big packet steamer leaving the lough on the first stage of its nightly trip to the busy port and rail terminus of Holyhead. The steamer was always packed with passengers and freight from the lush counties fringing the sea inlet, en route for Liverpool, London and other English and Welsh cities.

Exactly what happened in the darkness was never made clear but there was no hint that the collision, almost within hailing distance of the shore was due to any laxity on the part of the seamen who manned the ships. The night was bitterly cold and intermittently moonlit when black clouds were torn aside. A gale had blown for twenty-four hours, and if anything was getting worse as the *Connemara*, dead on time, left Greenore, moved cautiously into the channel and then between Haulbowline Lighthouse and the Cranfield shore towards Helly Hunter and The Whistler buoys to the open sea.

Crew and passengers numbered seventy-nine. She carried a cargo of prime cattle from the plains of Meath, other farm livestock and a mixed cargo of foodstuffs. When the big ship was squaring up for her five hour trip another vessel, the much smaller coasting steamer *Retriever* laden with Whitehaven coal was homing to the lough. Her crew of eleven included a ship's boy on his first working trip to sea. All were on watch as the collier faced the turbulence of the restricted channel. In the fashion of the little coal-burners she took all that wind and wave could throw at her.

It is thought that because of the high waves and the fact that for most of the time spray was being flung over her it may have been difficult to keep the *Retriever's* masthead lights functioning perfectly. There is a possibility too that as her bow was plunged into the waves the stern was clear of the water, her free propeller and rudder exercising the minimum influence on the steering. She may have yawed, sideslipped from a straight course, and been flung into the side of the big steamer. Whatever the cause she struck *Connemara* amidships tearing a jagged hole in the steel plates, and reared back, her own bows torn open. Water poured into both ships, bursting steam boilers adding to the speed with which they sank.

People on the shore knew nothing of what had happened so close to the beach but the flares sent up by the keepers of the Light on Haulbowline, in mid channel, indicated trouble. It was dawn before people on the beach had any idea of the extent of the horror. Since the moment of impact the tide had ebbed and flowed, and now was ebbing again. The sandy beach was littered for over a mile of its length with crates, barrels, wickerwork baskets, driftwood, drowned cattle and eighty dead bodies. Eight victims were never found. Among the men, women and children who lost their lives were soldiers returning to the Front after furloughs in Monaghan and Cavan.

A single small dinghy from the *Retriever*, half-full of water and on an even keel, was seen above the high watermark. Almost submerged, his legs jammed under the thwart (crossboard), was the body of the ship's boy. He was barely alive but after hours of care in a nearby cottage was able to tell something of what had happened. As the *Retriever* sank a shipmate had manhandled the little boat from the fo'c'sle head into the water and lowered the boy into it. The dinghy was tossed away into the darkness, the youngster, a non-swimmer, clinging desperately to it. Nobody else on either vessel survived. The young man who had launched the small boat, known as the strongest swimmer on the Mourne shore had somehow managed to make his way to the beach. He was found when the sun came up, above the line of breakers where he had dragged himself, almost unscathed. He died of exhaustion and exposure before help came.

There was much talk at school for pupils had lost relatives. Without mentioning it at home I agreed to accompany a classmate to the scene of the tragedy. We had never been more than half a mile along the coast in the direction of the lough mouth. By the time we had skirted the second cove we felt like turning back for the beach was rocky and slippery. It was desolate and lonely as we rounded the first headland and darkness was beginning to close in. We trudged on round another headland and saw a big crescent of sand and signs of activity half a mile away. On sighting the company we hurried, but after fifty yards drew up in desperate fright. Before us, on a patch of inblown weed, lay the body of a woman. Tendrils of sea whangs and broad blades of kelp covered most of her body. Her long hair spread on a mat of puffy bladder wrack.

We edged back and then, as if struck by a monstrous hand, turned together and ran to the grassy bank, then by the arrow-straight road to the coastal highway. We did not speak as we panted and strained to reach home, parted without a word, and tried to explain to our mothers something that was new and shocking in our lives. The shock and grief remained with us as it did with everybody in the town. On our way to and from school we saw the people coming from many different places to offer sympathy and support in the houses where the captain of the *Retriever*, his son and nephew, were being 'waked' together.

In the interval between Hallowe'en and Christmas our parents stocked up and made plans so that families could have the best possible fare at the end of the year. The carters and shopkeepers were planning too, bringing in cases of oranges, dried fruit and shiny red American apples for Christmas morning. The proprietors of the 'fancy goods' shops, where we bought our weekly magazines, also laid in extra goods, knowing there would be a demand for wax crayons, coloured pencils, india rubbers, the more expensive bound books, games of ludo and snakes and ladders, pencil cases with painted 'swing-off' tops, painted rubber balls, glassy marbles, and tops.

As the Feast approached we could see, looking into the bakery, men busy with the preparation of the currant loaves for which they were famous. These were heavy, rich, juicy, glazed, and so full of currants, sultanas, peel and citron that there seemed to be no room for the flour. If mother had been a good customer at the grocer's that year there was always a present of a currant loaf at Christmas, as well as bags of tea and sugar.

Puddings were made well in advance, for they took a lot of boiling. Before pressure cookers and steamers the biggest pot in the house had to be used over the open fire or on the range. When finished the puddings, in their cloths, were allowed to dry out before being hung away, out of the reach of children, like big cannonballs.

Chickens were in demand before Christmas but beef was by far the favourite constituent of the special meal. For people without ovens pot roasting was the cooking method adopted. There was a shortage of prime beef: to meet the demand the local butchers, who usually made meat deliveries round the country in horse-drawn carts, set up stalls along the side of the river brae displaying their wares and sawing, chopping and slicing busily until after dark when the country folk came in. By the light of hurricane lamps they stayed at work until all were satisfied.

Long after we knew that there was no visitor who came down the chimney, getting up by lamplight on Christmas morning was the peak of joy. There was always something for us: books, sweets, games, oranges and apples, things which made our day and gave us pleasure long afterwards. Nor did our winter pleasure end with Christmas if frosty weather, with a dusting of snow, blessed us in February. The wind from the east brought early darkness, but good conditions for preparing what was called the 'Slide' on the river brae. We carried buckets of water and poured it down the right-hand side of the hill so that, when it froze, there was a smooth sheet of ice from the top of the hill to the river wall itself. Youths from many parts came to show their skill, and some were experts, able to travel the whole length of the ice after a run of twenty yards on the flat.

Those who wore clogs had an advantage over the others, while some were expert at a kind of sliding called 'hunkering': after working up speed they dropped to their heels and, cutting out wind resistance, made swift descents. Others took red bricks from a pile by the store and used these as narrow toboggans, sitting on the bricks, and balancing with arms and legs spread. When those of us who were not night hawks had to leave, we could still hear the laughter and applause from the slide on the brae.

11

They Went to War

Much of our schoolwork entailed memorising facts. We steadily ploughed our way through lists of spellings, mathematical tables, all types of pronouns, adjectives and prepositions, the latter having been cleverly set out in a kind of rhyme. In the same way, by steady application, we built up a memory bank of poetry. We were required to stand up at the flick of the master's finger and recite our poems. The approach to geography was factual too and to this day I have not the slightest difficulty in naming, in a clockwise fashion, all the counties of Ireland and the shires and counties of England, Scotland and Wales, not to mention all the Irish towns and capes as well as islands and bays.

Quick pointing to places of importance on the Map of the World was an exercise we enjoyed and it certainly kept us awake. I knew where Vladivostock, Toulouse and Irkutsk were very early in life and could set a pointer on Galapagos, the Khyber Pass and the Hwang Ho in a split second. Our old, sagging map of Europe was just about ready for a facelift, or replacement, at the time when the power-hungry bosses of the Continent decided it was time the map was rolled up altogether and new national boundaries blocked in.

Our map-pointing exercises seldom took us in the direction of Montenegro and Serbia, though before our schooldays were over we knew about these places. The explosion detonated in that far part of the world and the news of the carnage that followed echoed even in our quiet backwater.

At first what was called 'the War' made little impact on us for we did not understand what it was all about. It was something that was happening very far away and newspaper reading was not as universal an exercise as it is now. Word-of-mouth comments from the readers were all we could expect and, anyway, we had a lot to do all day, every day. We listened in the cobbler's shop or in the saddler's as men argued about who was to blame, which leaders of the armies engaged were doing best, and whether or not the German submarines were likely to interfere with our fishing fleet. Our real interests in the saddler's shop were the cages of canaries and the cross-bred birds, called 'mules', that he reared.

In nearly all talk about the war the name 'Little Belgium' came up. We heard that Belgian refugees had come to stay and work in a private school just outside the town. Maybe we saw them, but if there was something different about either Belgians or refugees we did not notice it.

Gradually our interest in what was happening in France, and a place called Flanders, grew. The word that some men from our own town had been killed, but we had never known them. One of our coastal captains had his ship blown from under him off the south coast of Ireland by a German raider.

As far as our group was concerned the War really began when we awoke one morning to hear that most of our fishing luggers had been boarded by a crew from a German submarine, nearly twenty miles offshore, and had been sent to the bottom. We were well and truly in the war now. We saw men in uniform, sailors and soldiers, home on leave but as yet war games and guns did not figure in our play.

The news of something called a 'Rebellion' in Dublin reached us. As one of my friends in school was closely affected by it I was more interested than might have been expected. His mother, the Principal of the Infants' school, was caught in the Rising when she and her husband went to Dublin for a short holiday and there was anxiety for a few days until they managed to get out of the capital. As soon as they arrived home safely, however, we forgot about the Dublin affair, for we did not know much about the reasons for it.

Coloured posters on the walls urged men to join up, and we heard that some local men who had emigrated to America and Canada had come home to join the forces. We thought one of these young men was the best looking soldier we had ever seen. The son of a local schoolmaster, he had been in Canada for a couple of years before war broke out. He wore a kilt, a neat jacket and a coloured tartan over one shoulder. His buckled shoes suited his uniform and, best of all, he wore a dagger down the side of his stocking. After seeing him we tormented the old shoemaker for paper caps, like the Canadian Highlander wore, which he sometimes gave out to advertise rubber heels.

My outstanding memory of the War years, however, is of the day the soldiers' band came to town. We knew something was about to happen for preparations were made for speeches in front of the hotel. A platform was put up and on the day the band came it was crowded with men dressed in their best suits. Among them was a very old man with ribbons on his coat. We were told he had won them fighting in the Crimean War. Beside him was a younger, taller man who wore one medal we all knew. It was a V.C. and he had won it in the Boer War. Everything else was forgotten when we heard the band marching up the middle of the street. Even at the circus we had never seen such colour, strutting and flourishes. The music from the pipes of the Irish 'kilties' filled the street and was thrown back from the high houses.

The leader, a tall man made even taller by a big black hat, strode out in front of his green and saffron clad bandsmen as if he owned the town. He used his big leading stick as if it were as light as an eel clep. The bass drummer was also a massive man twirling his padded sticks nearly too fast for the eye to follow, and every now and then delighting us by swinging them behind his back to strike the drum without breaking the rhythm. The other drummers, drums hooked to their belts, worked as one, each stick rising and falling in unison, and every now and then putting the sticks to their lips.

When the pipers wailed to silence the marching tunes were taken up by rows of bandsmen behind with trumpets, clarinets and wide-mouthed brass horns that gave out notes of ground-shaking depth. The drummers in this section of the band were just as good as in the pipe section though they did not flourish their sticks with the same style. The sharp notes of flutes could be heard soaring above the brass instruments and giving a lightness to the tunes. When they drew up in front of the platform they joined in a number of tunes and we heard *The Minstrel Boy* and *Erin the Tear*, which we knew from school.

After the speeches the bands marched away and we saw some young men joining in to walk after them. We knew some of them and it seemed no time since they had been schoolboys.

After this we settled down to our normal way of life again. It was at this time I first heard the word 'margarine', but after the